C. Hart

Simpsons™ Comics

Jam-Packed Jamboree

A Division of Bongo Entertainment, Inc.

SIMPSONS COMICS JAM-PACKED JAMBOREE

Bongo Comics Group books may be purchased for educational, business,
or sales promotional use. For information, please call or write
P.O. Box 1963, Santa Monica, CA 90406-1963

FIRST EDITION

ISBN-10: 1-892849-14-3
ISBN-13: 978-1-892849-14-4

06 07 08 09 10 QWM 10 9 8 7 6 5 4 3 2 1

Publisher: MATT GROENING
Creative Director: BILL MORRISON
Managing Editor: TERRY DELEGEANE
Director of Operations: ROBERT ZAUGH
Art Director: NATHAN KANE
Art Director Special Projects: SERBAN CRISTESCU
Production Manager: CHRISTOPHER UNGAR
Legal Guardian: SUSAN A. GRODE

Trade Paperback Concepts and Design: SERBAN CRISTESCU

Contributing Artists:
KAREN BATES, TIM BAVINGTON, JOHN COSTANZA, LEA HERNANDEZ, JASON HO, NATHAN KANE,
OSCAR GONZALEZ LOYO, BILL MORRISON, KEVIN M. NEWMAN, PHYLLIS NOVIN, PHIL ORTIZ, RICK REESE,
MIKE ROTE, HORACIO SANDOVAL, STEVE STEERE, JR., CHRIS UNGAR, ART VILLANUEVA

Contributing Writers:
IAN BOOTHBY, ABBY DENSON, CHUCK DIXON, DAN FYBEL
JESSE LEON MCCANN, GAIL SIMONE

PRINTED IN CANADA

WILDERNESS GUIDE

IT'S JUDGEMENT DAY!
SIMPSONS COMICS
#64
US $2.50
CAN $3.50
ALL RISE FOR MARGE SIMPSON, TV'S LATEST JUDGE!
AND NOW, THE COURT FINDS IN FAVOR OF THIS IMPORTANT MESSAGE FROM OUR SPONSOR!

JUDGE MARGE

TO THE ***GALLOWS,*** KIRK VAN HOUTEN! FROM THERE YOU WILL BE DRAWN AND QUARTERED...

...ANY BODY PARTS STILL ***ALIVE*** WILL THEN FACE THREE CONSECUTIVE ***LIFE SENTENCES***.

IAN BOOTHBY
SCRIPT

OSCAR GONZALEZ LOYO
PENCILS

PHYLLIS NOVIN
INKS

ART VILLANUEVA
COLORS

KAREN BATES
LETTERS

BILL MORRISON
EDITOR

MATT GROENING
COURT REPORTER

THAT'S THE SENTENCE I WISH I COULD GIVE YOU DEADBEAT DADS!
BUT SINCE THIS IS A SMALL CLAIMS TV COURT, I FINE YOU $400.

HEH, HEH! I LOVE HOW JUDGE JULIE GOES AFTER LOUSY FATHERS WHO DON'T GIVE THEIR KIDS WHAT THEY NEED.
I STILL GET THE $500 FEE FOR APPEARING ON THE SHOW, RIGHT?
IX-NAY ON THE EE-FAY!

DAD, I NEED GLASSES!
HERE'S A PAIR I FOUND IN FLANDERS' TRASH!

WHAT'CHA GOT, LIS? LAZY EYE?
HARDLY. I HAVE WHAT MY OPTOMETRIST CALLS OVERACHIEVING EYE.

DAD, I CAN'T WEAR SOME-ONE ELSE'S GLASSES.
LISA, WE COULD FIGHT ALL DAY ABOUT THIS, OR WE COULD ASK THE MAGIC ANSWER BOX.
YOU MEAN THE TV?
SHHHH! IT'S TALKING.

HI, EVERYBODY!
HI, DR. NICK!

WELCOME TO MY PHONE IN SHOW WHERE I ANSWER ALL YOUR QUESTIONS ABOUT **MEDICALNESS** AND **DOCTOROLOGY**.

UH... DR. NICK?
SORRY.
NURSE SAMSON, PLEASE! I'M TRYING TO HOST A SHOW HERE.
BEEEEEEEEEEEEEEEEEEEP!

CALLER ONE, YOU ARE ON THE AIR!
HELLO, DR. NICK, I HAVE A QUESTION ABOUT GLASSES FOR MY DAUGHTER. ARE ALL PRESCRIPTIONS THE SAME?

EXCUSE ME. NURSE, COULD YOU TURN THAT HEART MONITOR OFF? THAT **LONG SUSTAINED BEEP** IS SO **ANNOYING** TO THE **EAR HOLES**!
BEEEEEEEEEEEEEEEEEEEP!

BUT BACK TO YOUR QUESTION. YES, ALL PRESCRIPTIONS ARE THE SAME. JUST LIKE DAILY WEAR THROWAWAY CONTACT LENSES WERE THE SAME AS THE REGULAR KIND.
IT'S ALL A BIG **EYE DOCTOR** SCAM.

SPEAKING OF SCAMS. FUNNY STORY. IT ALSO TURNS OUT **ALL KNOWN DISEASES** CAN BE CURED BY A SIMPLE **HOUSE-HOLD PRODUCT**.

STOP HIM! HE'LL RUIN US ALL!
THE PRODUCT IS...
NOOO!
WE WARNED YOU!

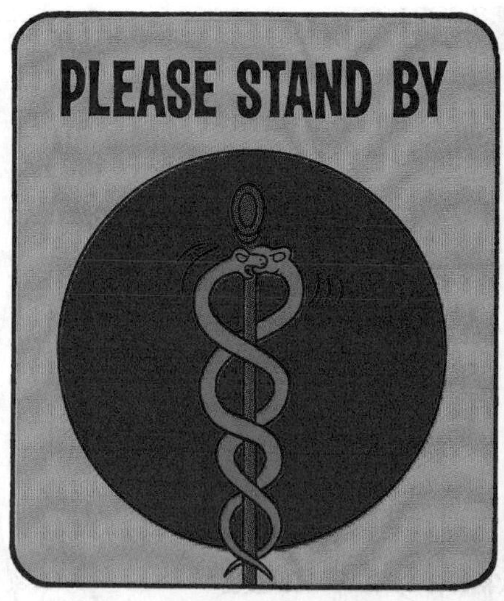
PLEASE STAND BY

SO YOU SEE LISA, THERE'S NO REASON TO BE AFRAID OF GETTING YOUR TONSILS OUT.
THIS IS ABOUT MY NEEDING GLASSES!

EWWW! YOU REALLY GOT THESE FROM MR. FLANDERS' TRASH?
IF BY "TRASH" YOU MEAN "FROM HIS FACE WHILE HE WAS ASLEEP IN HIS HAMMOCK," THEN YES.

MEANWHILE...
SCREEECH!
CRASH!
DADDY, SHOULD YOU BE DRIVING WITHOUT YOUR GLASSES?
BEING LEGALLY BLIND IS NO EXCUSE FOR MISSING CHURCH. FAITH WILL GUIDE US STRAIGHT AND TRUE!

HERE WE ARE!
UM... DADDY?
NO TIME TO TALK, ROD. YOU AND TODD GO GRAB A GOOD PEW WHILE I FIND A PARKING SPACE.
HARI KRISHNA TEMPLE
WELCOME ALL

LATER...
I GUESS I COULD AT LEAST TRY MR. FLANDERS' GLASSES.

AAAAAH!

IT'S LIKE MY EYES WERE SOAKED IN SUGAR!

WHAT'S ALL THE YELLING? DID NEW ZEALAND INVADE? I TRIED TO WARN THE PRESIDENT, BUT WOULD HE LISTEN?
SOCIAL
OH, HI, GRAMPA. I'M YELLING BECAUSE I NEED GLASSES FOR ONE OF MY EYES.

I MIGHT BE ABLE TO HELP.

YEP, HERE IT IS!

A MONOCLE? DID YOU GET THIS FROM A GERMAN OFFICER?
KINDA. I STOLE IT FROM WERNER KLEMPERER'S DRESSING ROOM WHEN I WAS A SECURITY GUARD FOR TV'S "HOGAN'S HEROES."

OH MY GOSH! I CAN SEE PERFECTLY. THANKS, GRAMPA.

YAAA!
SHUDDER!

NO OFFENSE, ABE, BUT YOUR GRANDDAUGHTER LOOKS DURNED CREEPY WITH THAT THING.
RIGHT, AND YOUR COLOSTOMY BAG MAKES YOU A REGULAR TICKLE ME ELMO.

YOU KNOW, BOYS, I THINK IT'S GREAT THAT AFTER ALL THESE YEARS REVEREND LOVEJOY ISN'T AFRAID TO TRY NEW THINGS.
DOES ANYONE WANT THE REST OF MY CHICKPEA SALAD?
MY HEAD ITCHES.

CRASH!
WHAT THE...?

WHEW! THANK THE LORD WE GOT THOSE "PRAYER" BAGS INSTALLED. NOW READ THE BIBLE VERSES WHILE I TALK TO THE NICE PERSON WE HIT.
YES, DADDY!
Then Jesus went into
In the beginning

SORRY, SORRY! ALL MY FAULT! I HOPE YOU HAVE AN AIRBAG IN THERE WITH YOU.

WHAT DID HE CALL ME?
I'LL TAKE CARE OF IT, MOTHER.
GUT HIM LIKE A TROUT!

GOOD TO SEE YOU, OFFICER! THIS MAN STRUCK MY CAR!
IT'S TRUE! I DID!
WELL, THERE'S NOTHING I CAN DO ABOUT IT. COURT'S CLOSED UNTIL JUDGE SNYDER COMES BACK FROM SICK LEAVE.

WHAT'S WRONG WITH HIM?

"HE GOT THAT LYME DISEASE THAT'S BEEN GOING AROUND."
I'LL BE HONEST, THOSE FLEAS ARE WAY TOO EXPENSIVE FOR A GUY LIKE ME, BUT THESE DEER TICKS ARE JUST AS GOOD. RIGHT, FOLKS?
GIL'S FLEA CIRC
C'MON, CROWD IN FOR A CLOSER LOOK!

SO A MAN CAN'T EVEN GET JUSTICE IN THIS TOWN ANYMORE?
GUESS NOT.
WELL, **THIS WILL NOT STAND!**

I WANT YOU TO TAKE THIS CHALK AND WRITE "I WILL BE A BETTER DRIVER" **ONE HUNDRED TIMES** ON THE ROAD.
OKILLY DOKILLY!

DID YOU SEE THAT?
WHAT **DECISIVE ACTION!**
I WIL

HEY, WHY NOT LET **HIM** BE THE NEW JUDGE?
ME? WELL, I...
WILL YA, MISTER? WE REALLY NEED TO START **PROSECUTING** AGAIN.

THE POLICE CAR IS GETTING PRETTY **FULL**.
THIS IS LIKE, TOTALLY BAD FOR MY **SCIATICA**.

AS LONG AS IT'S AFTER SCHOOL HOURS OR ON WEEKENDS, I'LL DO IT!
YAY!
HUZZAH!
HOORAY!
BOOOOOOO!

WHAT?

THE NEXT DAY...
HEY, LISA! GIMME YOUR LUNCH MONEY!

I WILL NOT. I NEED THAT MONEY FOR A WELL-BALANCED MEAL!

O-OKAY LISA! WE DON'T WANT ANY TROUBLE! LET'S GET OUTTA HERE!

HMMMMM.

MEANWHILE...
NOW, SOME OF YOU MAY BE ASKING WHY WE'RE IN THE MALL FOOD COURT. THE REAL COURT WAS RENTED OUT FOR BINGO THIS WEEK, AND WE COULDN'T AFFORD TO GIVE THE DEPOSIT BACK.
FIRST UP, SNAKE. YOU ARE ACCUSED OF CAR THEFT. HOW DO YOU PLEAD?
I'VE NEVER STOLEN A CAR IN MY LIFE, DUDE!

THEN WHY ARE YOU MR. JUNE IN THE NEW CAR THIEF SWIMSUIT CALENDAR?
MMMM...MMMM. HE'S GRAND THEFT AUTO-EROTIC!

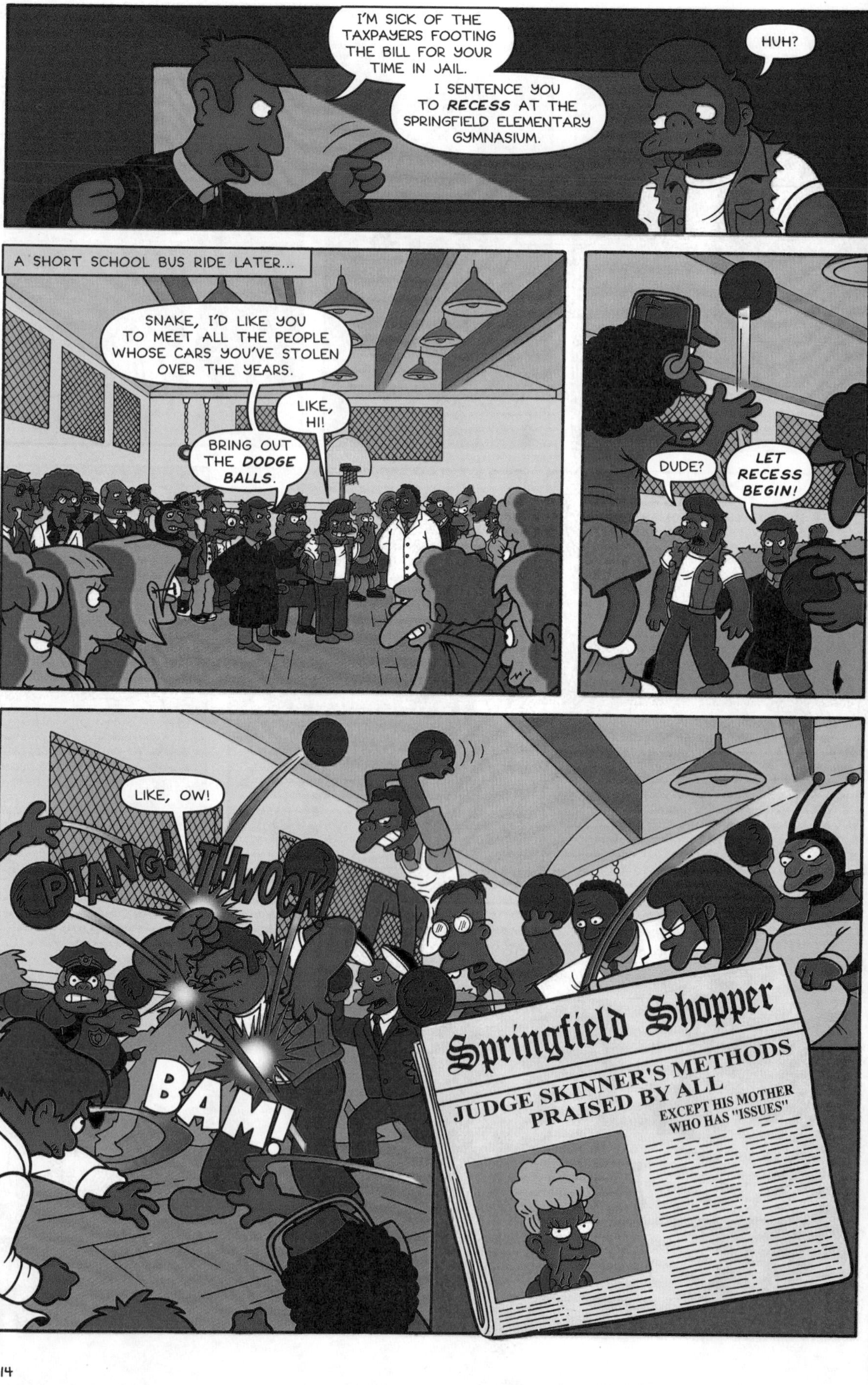

LIKE, OW!

PTANG! THWOCK!

BAM!

Springfield Shopper

JUDGE SKINNER'S METHODS PRAISED BY ALL

EXCEPT HIS MOTHER WHO HAS "ISSUES"

LISA'S HALLOWEEN CANDY MUST BE AROUND HERE SOMEWHERE.
LET'S SEE, IF I WAS A VEGETARIAN, STRAIGHT "A", JAZZ FAN, WHERE WOULD I HIDE MY ALMOND JOYS AND SNICKER-DOODLES?

AHEM!

GASP!

OH, HI, LISA. I WAS JUST...
...REMAKING YOUR BED. THOSE HOSPITAL CORNERS CAN'T BE TOO TIGHT, YOU KNOW.

WELL, GOTTA GO.
LEAP!

WHAAAA?

AAAAAAAAAAAAAHH!

DAD SAWED OFF THE ESCAPE BRANCH FROM THE TREE LAST SUMMER, REMEMBER?
OH, RIGHT.

THE NEXT DAY...
GET YOUR FREE SAMPLE OF OUR NEW ORGANIC FRUIT SNACKS!
I'D LIKE AN ORGANIC FRUIT SNACK.

TAKE THEM ALL, JUST DON'T HURT ME!

THIS MONOCLE SEEMS TO BRING WITH IT RESPECT AND FEAR. BUT I CAN'T LET IT GO TO MY HEAD.

I WANT FREE SAMPLES, AND I WANT THEM NOW!
SNAP!
YES, MA'AM!

WE'LL BE BROADCASTING YOUR NEXT FEW CASES LIVE ON THE NEWS, TO SEE IF YOU'RE READY TO HAVE YOUR OWN TV SERIES.
LIKE JUDGE JULIE?
HER SHOW'S BEEN PUT ON HIATUS.

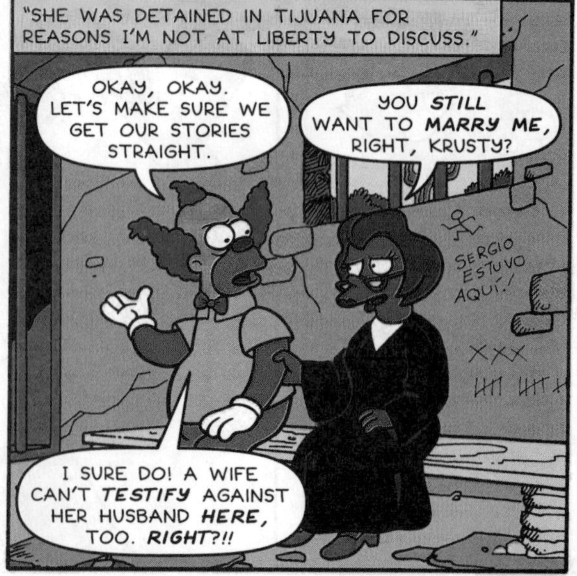
"SHE WAS DETAINED IN TIJUANA FOR REASONS I'M NOT AT LIBERTY TO DISCUSS."
OKAY, OKAY. LET'S MAKE SURE WE GET OUR STORIES STRAIGHT.
YOU STILL WANT TO MARRY ME, RIGHT, KRUSTY?
SERGIO ESTUVO AQUI!
I SURE DO! A WIFE CAN'T TESTIFY AGAINST HER HUSBAND HERE, TOO. RIGHT?!!

NOW REMEMBER, PEOPLE ARE CRAZY ABOUT YOUR UNFLAPPABLE DISCIPLINARIAN THING.
KEEP THAT UP, AND YOU'LL BE A STAR!

HEAR ME, HEAR ME! COURT IS NOW IN SESSION! FIRST CASE ON THE DOCKET IS...
WHACK!

WHAT'S UP, DOCKET?
AAAAAH!

BART!
PRINCIPAL SKINNER, WHAT ARE YOU DOING IN YOUR MOTHER'S DRESS?

I'LL HAVE YOU KNOW THIS IS MY DRESS!
HA, HA!
I MEAN MY ROBE! I MEAN, STOP SKATEBOARDING IN MY COURT!

HE'S LOST CONTROL OF HIS OWN COURT!
NO ONE CAN STOP THAT WILD CHILD!
ALL IS LOST!

BART!
GULP!

YOU STOP BOTHERING JUDGE SKINNER, RIGHT NOW!
OR WHAT?

OR I'LL SHOW YOUR BABY PICTURES TO THE TV CAMERAS UNTIL YOU STOP!
NOOOOOO!

IT'S OVER! I'M DONE! I APOLOGIZE FOR THIS HORRIBLE MISUNDERSTANDING. JUST PUT THE PICTURES AWAY!

WELL DONE, WELL DONE. HUMILIATION, JUSTICE, PLUS A TOUCH OF NUDITY. I LOVE IT!
I WANT TO OFFER YOU YOUR OWN SHOW AS A TV JUDGE.

A JUDGE? I DON'T KNOW. I'VE BEEN ARRESTED... TWICE. IN FACT, EVERY MEMBER OF MY FAMILY HAS, EXCEPT FOR MAGGIE BECAUSE SHE WAS TOO YOUNG TO BE TRIED FOR ATTEMPTED MURDER.
I LOVE IT! IT GIVES YOU AN EDGE.
BUT WHAT ABOUT ME?

The Springfield Shopper
"JUDGE" MARGE TO HOST OWN SHOW
WIMPY SKINNER'S MOTHER WAS RIGHT AFTER ALL

THAT NIGHT...
MARGE, WHAT IF AFTER YOU BECOME A JUDGE, YOU **CHANGE**?
OH, I'LL STILL BE THE SAME. NOW GO TO SLEEP.

GOOD **POST-APOCALYPTIC** MORNING TO YOU, MARGE!
WHAT'S FOR BREAKFAST?

THAT'S JUDGE MARGE TO YOU, **CITIZEN!** AND I AM **THE LAW!**
YOU ARE CHARGED WITH DRINKING MILK FROM THE ELECTRO-CARTON, EXCESSIVE NAPPING ON THE CYBER-COUCH, AND LEAVING THE SEAT UP ON THE RECYCLO-TOILET!

HOW DO YOU **PLEAD**?
I...

GUILTY AS CHARGED!
ZAP!

OH, AND DON'T FORGET TO PICK THE KIDS UP FROM **BIG BROTHER'S UNLEARNING ACADEMY**.
YES, DEAR.

THE NEXT DAY...
YOU ARE CHARGED WITH **SECOND-DEGREE MEGALOMANIACAL WORLD DOMINATION**. HOW DO YOU PLEAD, DR. COLOSSUS?
TSK! TSK!
DO WE HAVE TO HAVE MY MOTHER HERE SAYING, "TSK! TSK!"? IT'S UNNERVING.

WELL, YOU SHOULD HAVE THOUGHT OF THAT BEFORE ALL YOUR CRIMINAL MASTERMINDING!
FINE! FINE! I CONFESS! JUST STOP THE SCOLDING!

FANTASTIC WORK TODAY, MARGE! YOUR NELSON RATINGS ARE THROUGH THE ROOF!
YOU MEAN NIELSEN RATINGS.

NO, I MEAN NELSON.
YOU KICK BUTT!

THE NIELSEN FAMILY DIED OFF YEARS AGO DUE TO INBREEDING. NOW WE RELY ON SMALL CHILDREN, THE ELDERLY, AND THE OCCASIONAL ESCAPED MENTAL PATIENT FOR RATINGS.
SUDDENLY, TELE-VISION MAKES A LOT MORE SENSE.

MEANWHILE...
HEY, HOMER. YOU EVER NOTICE WHEN MOM GETS A JOB THINGS FALL APART HERE AT HOME?
YES. YES I HAVE. I MEAN, NORMALLY LISA HELPS OUT AS THE VOICE OF REASON, BUT LATELY...

I'M TAKING YOUR PIGGY BANK AND GOING SHOPPING. ANY OBJECTIONS?
NO, LISA.
GOOD. CARRY ON.

ANYWAY, I FELT WE COULD USE AN AUTHORITY FIGURE, SO THE HOUSE DOESN'T GET CONDEMNED AGAIN.
BUT WHO, BART? WHO?

JUDGE SNYDER! HE'S HEALTHY AGAIN, AND NOW THAT MOM'S TAKEN OVER, HE'S OUT OF WORK.
HOW DID I MISS HIM STANDING RIGHT THERE?
I'VE BEEN A FAMILY COURT JUDGE FOR TWENTY YEARS. I'LL WORK FOR FOOD.
YOU'RE HIRED. NOW QUIT BLOCKING THE TV, YOUR HONOR!

YOU KNOW, I REALLY WOULD LIKE TO GET OUT OF HERE *EARLY* AND GET MY GROCERY SHOPPING DONE. WOULD YOU MIND CONFESSING? IT'D REALLY *HELP ME OUT*.
I DON'T WANNA.

CAN YOU REALLY LOOK *BAILIFF MAGGIE* IN THE EYE AND SAY YOU DIDN'T ROB THAT BANK?

I DID IT! I DID IT!

USING BABIES FOR CONFESSIONS.
WHEN I THINK OF ALL THE TIME I WASTED WITH PHONEBOOKS, RUBBER HOSES, AND PILLOW CASES FULL OF SOAP BARS.
WAY TO GO, JUDGE MARGE!
YAY!

MEANWHILE...
IF IT PLEASES THE COURT, I'D LIKE TO SUBMIT THESE PHOTOS AS EXHIBIT "A".
SO ENTERED.
A

THESE PHOTOS CLEARLY SHOW ONE HOMER J. SIMPSON **STEALING MY DESSERT**!
WHY YOU LITTLE...!

I WARNED YOU, MR. SIMPSON! ONE MORE **CHOKING RELATED OUT-BURST,** AND YOU'D BE HELD IN CONTEMPT!
BUT THE BOY...
GAAK!

TAKE HIM AWAY!
WHERE DID **YOU** COME FROM?
TEMP AGENCY.

SIGH I MISS MARGE.

FOR BREAKING AND ENTERING PLUS MAKING THE BAILIFF CRY, I GROUND YOU FOR TWO YEARS! NO DESSERTS OR CABLE TV!
I THINK YOU NEED A **TIME OUT** TO THINK ABOUT WHAT YOU'VE DONE.
NO! JUST SEND ME TO **PRISON**!

ORDER IS BEING MAINTAINED. EXCELLENT. NOW FOR A GOOD TOOTH BRUSHING AND THEN TO THE MALL.

I'LL JUST TAKE OUT THE MONOCLE, AND...
WHAT?
NO!

NEVER TAKE IT OUT! THE MONOCLE IS FEAR! THE MONOCLE IS POWER!
BUT, DO I WANT PEOPLE TO FEAR ME?

DUH! LOOK AT ALL THE STUFF YOU GOT TODAY! AND THERE'S MORE TO COME!
HOW MUCH MORE?

NO! THIS IS WRONG! THE POWER IS CORRUPTING ME!

THIS ENDS NOW!
NOOOOOOO!

LISA, GREAT NEWS! THE WERNER KLEMPERER FAN CLUB CALLED ME. THEY'RE OFFERING $50,000 FOR THE MONOCLE.
D'OH!

LATER THAT NIGHT AT THE (FOOD) COURT...
CAN'T WE WRAP IT UP NOW? I'M EXHAUSTED AND I MISS MY FAMILY.
NO! WE OWN YOU, MARGE. IN FACT, WE'D LIKE YOU TO START SLEEPING IN YOUR TRAILER INSTEAD OF GOING HOME AT NIGHT.
NOW FOR THE NEXT CASE...
Z Z Z

WHAT THE...
MARGE, HONEY, WE NEED YOU BACK!
4.95

THE PLACE IS A **MESS**. I'M UNDER **HOUSE ARREST** AND CAN'T LEAVE HOME WITHOUT WEARING THIS **LEG BAND** THAT SHOCKS ME EVERY TWENTY SECONDS.

AAAAAH!

BART'S RUNNING THINGS, AND LISA'S UNDER A MONOCLE'S **EVIL POWER**.

NO, I'M NOT. I GOT OVER THAT **THIS AFTERNOON**.
WELL, THANKS FOR **KEEPING ME IN THE LOOP**. NOW I LOOK LIKE AN **IDIOT**.

AAAAAH!

OH, HOMER! I WISH I **COULD** QUIT, BUT THEY HAVE ME UNDER **CONTRACT**. THEY COULD **SUE**!

UM...MOM, YOU SIGNED THIS CONTRACT "JUDGE MARGE." IF YOU'RE NOT A JUDGE ANYMORE, IT'S **NOT VALID**.
I QUIT!
RRIP!

WAIT! YOU CAN'T!
BUT ONE FINAL JUDICIAL ACT! YOU'RE HELD **IN CONTEMPT** UNTIL I'M GONE!
COME ALONG YOU!
ALL RIGHT!
WAY TO GO MARGE!

NOW, LET'S ALL GET SOME ICE CREAM!
YAY!

SO, JUDGE SNYDER'S BEING REINSTATED RIGHT NOW?
YEP, AND AS A FORMER JUDGE, I HAVE A GET OUT OF JAIL FREE CARD.
OH, HOW CUTE. LIKE MONOPOLY. HEY, WAIT! THIS IS REAL.

AAAAAH!

ARE YOU OKAY, HOMEY?
YEAH, THE POLICE SAID THEY'D TAKE THE LEG BAND OFF WITHIN FIVE BUSINESS DAYS. THE ICE CREAM STOPS THE INTERNAL ELECTRICAL BURNS PRETTY GOOD, THOUGH.

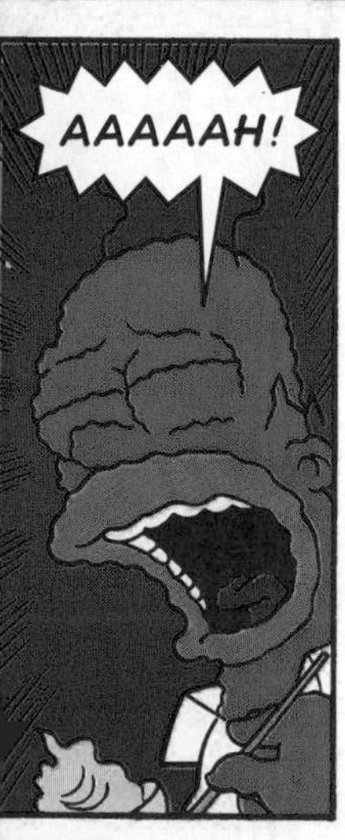
AAAAAH!

WELL, YOU KNOW WHAT THEY SAY. "I SCREAM, YOU SCREAM, WE ALL SCREAM FOR ICE CREAM." HEE, HEE!

C'MON, MOM. DAD'S REALLY SUFFERING.
YOU'RE RIGHT. I'M SORRY.

AAAAAH!

HA! HA! HA! HA! HA!
THE END

COMICS BONGO GROUP
MALIBU
Stacy
APPROVED BY THE COMICS CODE AUTHORITY
NO. 1
$2.50
I'M FREEZING, MALIBU STACY! DO WE HAVE TO WEAR BIKINIS?
COME ON, MUFFY! A BEACH IS A BEACH!
?
A PETROCHEM PETROCHEMICAL PUBLICATION
MATT GROENING

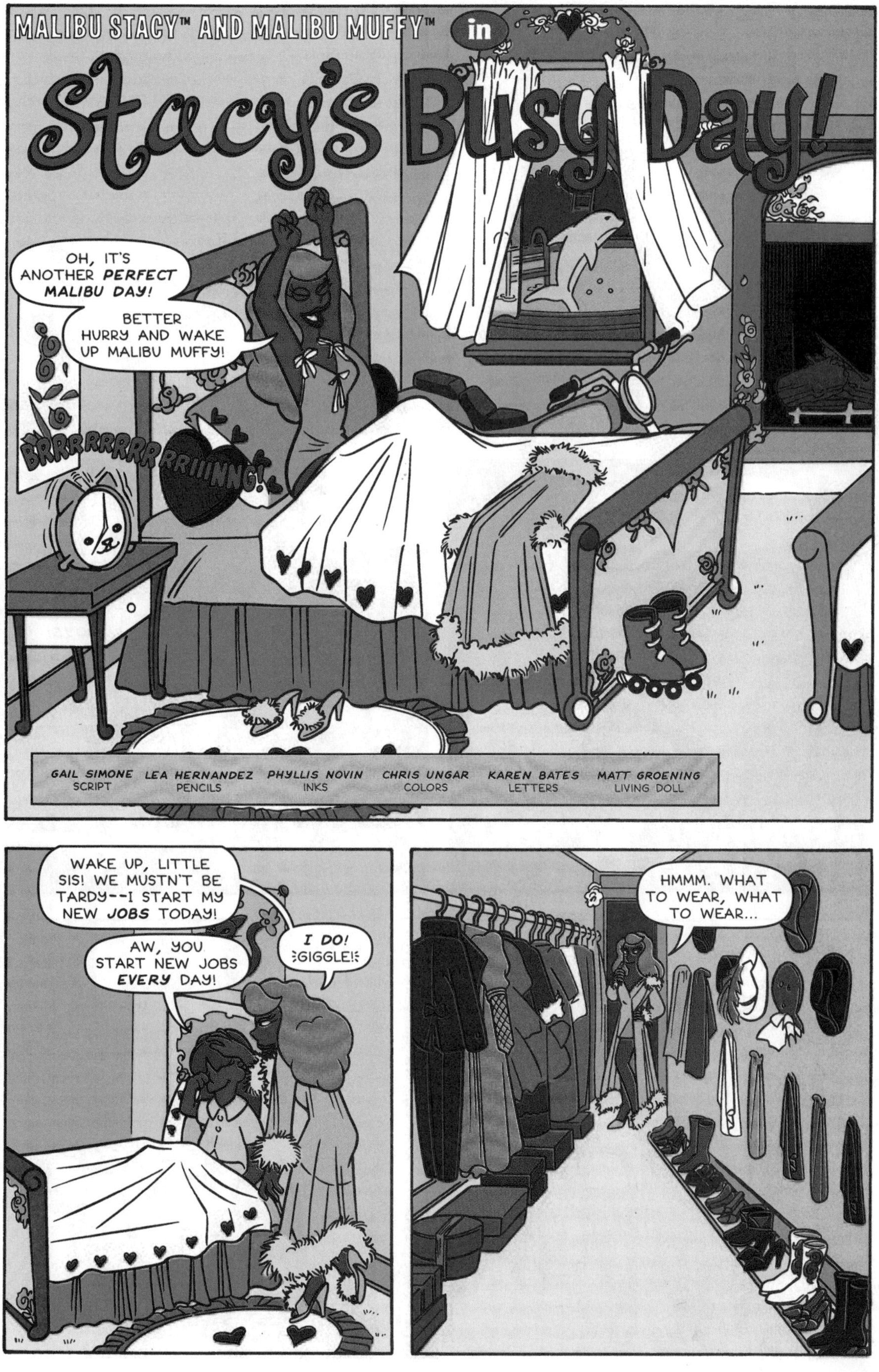

MALIBU STACY™ AND MALIBU MUFFY™ in

Stacy's Busy Day!

OH, IT'S ANOTHER ***PERFECT MALIBU DAY!***

BETTER HURRY AND WAKE UP MALIBU MUFFY!

BRRRRRRRRRRRRIIINNG!

GAIL SIMONE SCRIPT · **LEA HERNANDEZ** PENCILS · **PHYLLIS NOVIN** INKS · **CHRIS UNGAR** COLORS · **KAREN BATES** LETTERS · **MATT GROENING** LIVING DOLL

AREN'T YOU EATING, STACY?
I'M NOT VERY HUNGRY THIS WEEK, MUFFY. BUT YOU ENJOY!
COOKING IS IMPORTANT FOR GIRLS TO LEARN...

...ESPECIALLY IF THEY WANT TO CATCH A HUSBAND!
OH, MUFFY! DON'T BE SILLY! TODAY'S WOMAN DOESN'T HAVE TO BE A HOUSEWIFE! LOOK, THESE ARE JUST THE JOBS I START TODAY!

I FEEL LIKE I'VE LOST EIGHTY-SIX POUNDS AND THREE OUNCES!
ASTRO-NAVIGATION IS HARD!
ASTRONAUT STACY™!

GO, TEAM! PUT THAT...BALL THING...WHEREVER IT GOES! RAH! RAH!
SPORTS ARE FOR BOYS!
CHEERLEADER STACY™!

THIS PATIENT NEEDS 10 CCS OF SOME SORT OF DRUGS OR SOME-THING, STAT!
GOING TO THE MALL IS FUN!
NEUROSURGEON STACY™!

...AND THAT'S WHY I VOTE FOR CHOCOLATE AND AGAINST CALORIES!
ROLLER-BLADING RULES!
SUPREME COURT JUSTICE STACY™!

Well, we've got lots of letters in our mailbag this month, so let's get right to them, shall we?

Dear Malibu Stacy,
Congratulations on another fabulous issue. I must admit, the suspense when Malibu Tad asked you if you'd go to the big dance was unbearable! Kudos to the entire crew at *Malibu Stacy Comics* for their masterful story-telling.

However, I do have one small complaint...on page one of "*Stacy's Beach Brunch Bunch*," the dots on her fashionable two-piece swimsuit are light red--and yet, just a page later, they're dark pink. How could this be?

I'm pleasingly puzzled!

Your biggest fan,
Waylon Smithers

Well, I must say, you certainly ***ARE*** *a sharp-eyed little girl! However, it's easy to explain. I got a little bit of nasty ol' sand on my suit, so, of course, I had to run and change! But thanks for paying such close attention to my stories, and congratulations to your parents for giving you such an unusual and charming name!*

Dear Malibu Stacy,
I'm in fourth grade. There's this boy I like, but I'm not sure if he likes me. What should I do?

Tina Pemberton

This one's easy! Simply find out what this boy likes, and completely change your likes and personality to match his. Some of the best solutions are the simplest ones! Let me know how it turns out, Tina!

Dear Malibu Stacy,
I'm eight years old, and I go to Springfield Elementary. I love your adventures and your carefree attitude. I've drawn a picture of you, which I've included.

Lisa Simpson

P.S. If this is considered trespassing on your copyrighted image, please forgive me, as I am unaware of the legal consequences.

Dear Lisa,

I would never wear green with orange.

Well, that's all for this month! Join us next month for my next thrilling adventure, "Never Enough Shoes!"

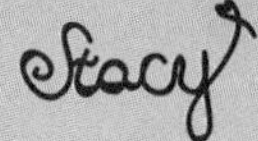

KIDS! ASK YOUR MOM TO HELP YOU CUT THESE OUT! HERE I AM WEARING SOME OUTFITS FROM SOME OF MY ALL-TIME FAVORITE FILMS!
MALIBU Stacy™
IN
FILM FASHIONS
SPACE PRINCESS!
GLADIATOR GIRL!
CROSS-DRESSING SCIENTIST!

DING DONG!
DOORBELL! IT'S PROBABLY *TAD* PICKING YOU UP FOR YOUR *DATE,* STACY!
OH, NO! HE CAN'T SEE ME LIKE *THIS!* STALL HIM WHILE I GO CHANGE!

STACY! IT'S NOT TAD! IT'S YOUR FRIENDS: *AFRICAN AMERICAN STACY™, NATIVE AMERICAN STACY™, AND ASIAN STACY™!*
HI, MUFFY!

NOT SO *FAST,* MUFFY! I'M HERE, TOO! IS MALIBU STACY READY TO GO ON OUR *BIG DATE?*
HI, TAD!

HELLO, *TAD.*

STACY... YOU... ...YOU LOOK *BEAUTIFUL!*

I KNOW.

THE WELL-DRESSED ***END!***

JOIN THE FIESTA!
SIMPSONS
COMICS
#65
US $2.50
CAN $3.50
MATT GROENING
ROCKET

CHUCK DIXON
STORY

HORACIO SANDOVAL
PENCILS

ART VILLANUEVA
COLORS

STEVE STEERE, JR.
INKS

KAREN BATES
LETTERS

BILL MORRISON
EDITOR

MATT GROENING
BENEVOLENT DICTATOR

EAT MORE OFTEN
HAND IT OVER!
NO WAY!
GIMME!
UNNH-UH!

HELLO? AGITATED CONVENIENCE STORE OWNER WITH ITCHY TRIGGER FINGER? NEED I SAY MORE?
Duff

BUT IT'S THE LAST SIX PACK OF DUFF, APU!
AND I SAW IT FIRST.
Duff
Duff
DRINK SODA

I MUST BLAME MYSELF, LOYAL CUSTOMERS.
I UNDERESTIMATED THE THIRST OF THE TEACHER'S UNION CONVENTION MEETING IN TOWN THIS WEEK.

I GUESS WE COULD SPLIT IT...
DRINK Duff
SURE, WE'RE PALS, HOMER.

BARNEY! LOOK!
THE DUFF TRUCK!
SWEET DELIVERANCE!

WHERE IS IT?
DRINK Duff
YOINK!

ONE SIX PACK TO GO, APU!
HA HA HA!
NO

YOU'LL BE SORRY, HOMER!
DON'T THINK SO!
HEE HEE HEE HEE HEE!

YOU WON'T ENJOY THAT BEER! IT'LL BRING YOU NOTHING BUT MISERY! IT'LL BE FLAT AND TASTELESS, AND YOU'LL REGRET THIS DAY!
ITS FOAMY GOODNESS WILL TURN TO POISON IN YOUR MOUTH.

GUG GUG GUG GUG

MMM...PURE AMBROSIA.
MAN, NOTHING ON TV. SUNDAY AFTER-NOONS BITE.
Duff

HEY, HOMER. YOU SEE THIS CONTEST? TWO WEEKS IN A TROPICAL PARADISE.
YOU DRAIN PLENTY OF BREWSKIS. MAYBE YOU COULD WIN.
DUFF'S CARIBBEAN ESCAPE! YOU COULD BE A WINNER!
Duff Beer
Duff BEER

NAW...THOSE CONTESTS ARE ALL SO PHONY. NOBODY ACTUALLY WINS THEM.
WHAT KIND OF LOSER BUYS BEER JUST TO WIN A CONTEST?

AWW...
NO BALMY TROPICAL BREEZES FOR GIL...
Be a Winner
Duff
Duff
Duff
Duff
Duff
Duff

CAN I HAVE THE CAP, DAD?
SURE, SON. I REMEMBER SNIFFING BEER CAPS WHEN I WAS A BOY.
GOLDEN DAYS...

WHOA-HO!
HOLD ON TO YOUR BLADDER, HOMEBOY. WE WON.
WINNER!

SPHHHHHHT!
HEY!

?
WOO-HOO!
?

SOON...
DUFF BEER IS PROUD TO ANNOUNCE THE WINNER OF OUR CARIBBEAN ESCAPE!
A MAN WHO KNOWS THE FROSTY AMBER GOODNESS OF DUFF AND DRINKS A LOT OF IT!
THAT'S ME!
Duff
1 SIMPSONS Duff

YOU AND YOUR FAMILY WILL SPEND TWO WEEKS ON SANDY BEACHES UNDER A TROPICAL SUN THANKS TO DUFF!
WOW. BIG TICKETS.
1 SIMPSONS Duff
TO SYMBOLIZE THE BIG FUN YOU'LL BE HAVING!

Duff
SIMPSONS Duff
BOSQUEVERDE? BUT ISN'T THAT PLACE A GODAWFUL--

--FULLY WONDERFUL PARADISE ISLAND OF BEAUTY AND JOY?
YOU BET, LITTLE GIRL!
Duff

WHO SAYS DRINKING BEER TO WIN A CONTEST MAKES YOU A LOSER?
YOU DID, DAD.

IN YOUR FACE!
Duff

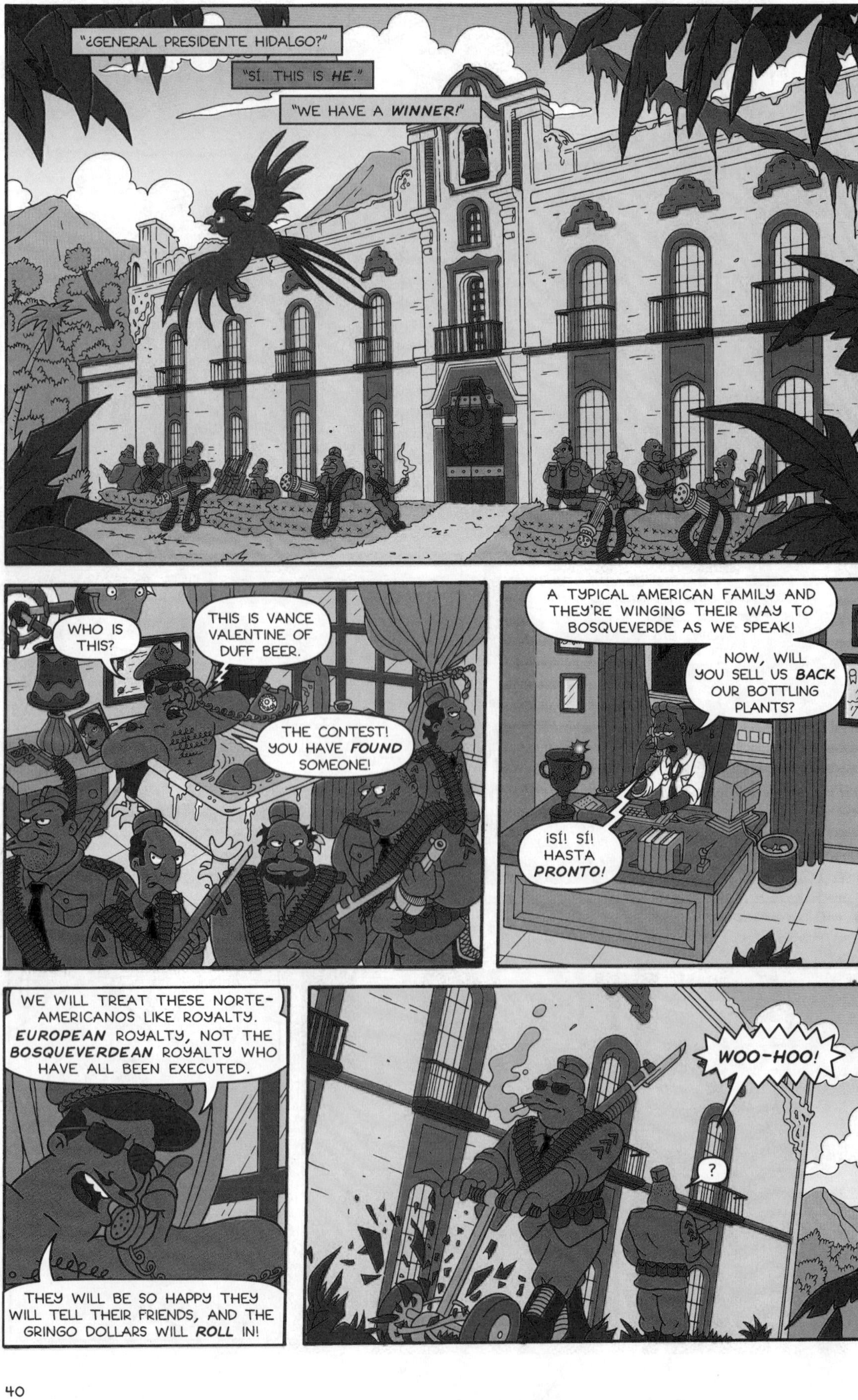

"¿GENERAL PRESIDENTE HIDALGO?"

"SÍ. THIS IS *HE*."

"WE HAVE A ***WINNER!***"

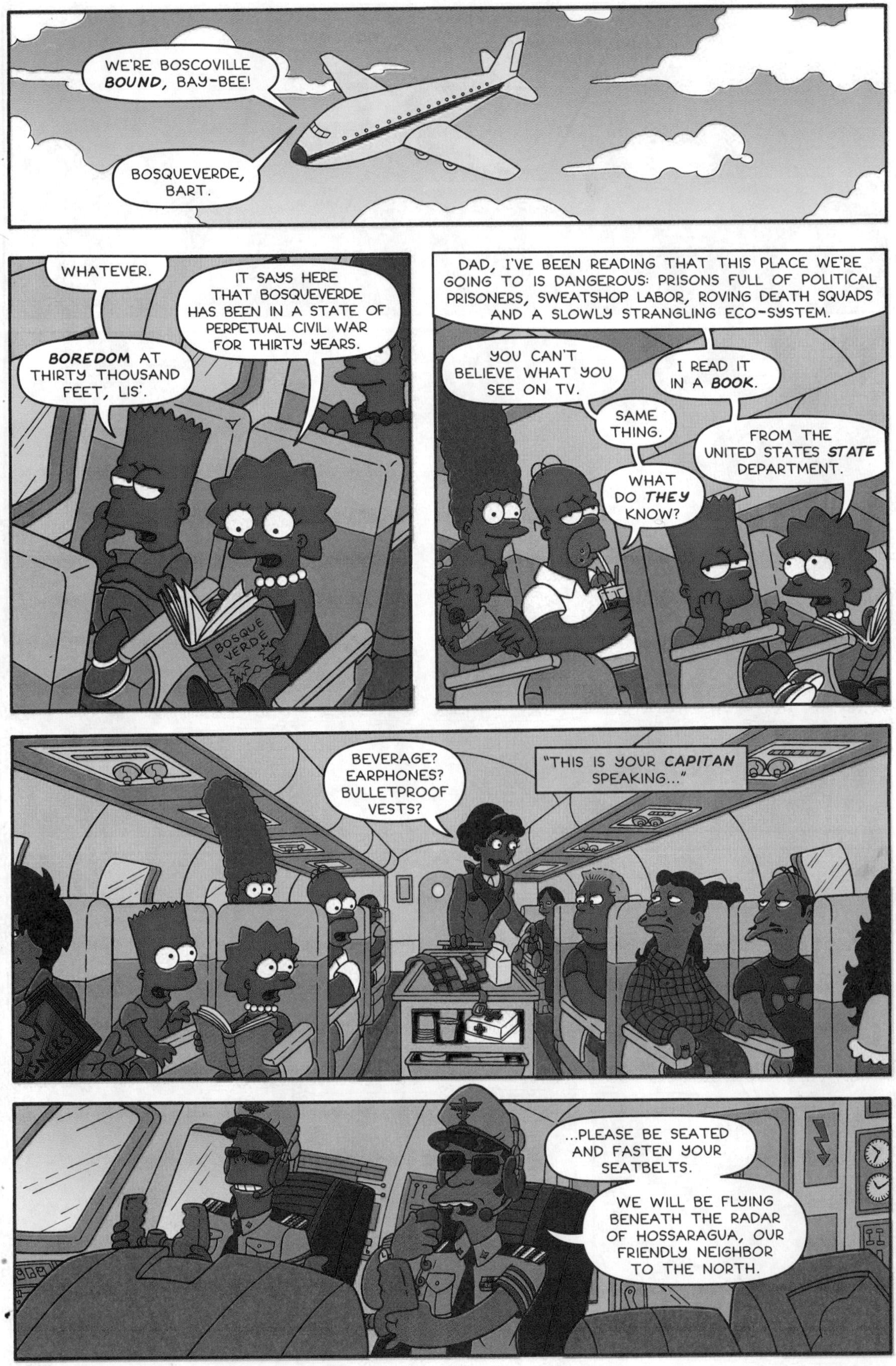

BEVERAGE? EARPHONES? BULLETPROOF VESTS?

"THIS IS YOUR ***CAPITAN*** SPEAKING..."

...PLEASE BE SEATED AND FASTEN YOUR SEATBELTS.

WE WILL BE FLYING BENEATH THE RADAR OF HOSSARAGUA, OUR FRIENDLY NEIGHBOR TO THE NORTH.

THE SIMPSONS! WELCOME TO MY HOMELAND!
HOW WAS YOUR FLIGHT?

JUST FINE EXCEPT FOR LANDING ON A HIGHWAY.
LO SIENTO, SEÑORA. THERE WAS A LITTLE ACCIDENT AT THE AIRPORT.
BUT THAT WILL NOT SPOIL YOUR TRIP, EH?

YEAH! I CAN'T WAIT TO GET TO OUR LUXURY HOTEL!
I AM SORRY BUT THERE WAS ALSO A REGRETTABLE ACCIDENT AT THE HOTEL.
YOU WILL BE STAYING AT MY HOUSE.

THERE ARE FIVE POOLS, A RIDING RING, GOLF COURSE, AND TENNIS COURTS.
WOW...
YOU ARE FREE TO USE ALL OF THEM AS MY GUESTS.
COOL!

I HAVE JUST... ***MOVED*** IN. THE PLACE REALLY ISN'T "ME" YET.
THIS MUST BE THE BIGGEST HOUSE IN THE ***WORLD***.

SADLY, THAT IS NOT TRUE, NIÑO.
THERE IS ANOTHER, MUCH ***LARGER*** HOUSE.

¿DAQUIRI, SEÑOR?

ARE YOU MARRIED, GENERAL?
AH, SÍ. MY WIFE WILL BE IN AFTER SHE IS FINISHED ***SINGING*** ON THE BALCONY.

♪ DON'T CRY FOR ME, BOSQUEVERDE. ♫ YOUR TEARS MEAN NOTHING TO ME. I WONDER WHYYYYY EVERY NIIIGHT– ♪ YOU COME TO SEEEE ME. ♪

♪ WE HAVE NO TEE-VEEEEEE... ♫

PICA Y RASCA
MI JUNTA ES SU JUNTA

¡ATENCIÓN, CIÚDADANOS! ¡ESCÚCHENME!

¡SOY EL PRESIDENTE VITALICIO, RASCA!

¿SEÑOR PRESIDENTE? ¿PODRIA POSAR PARA UN RETRATO?
¡ME GUSTARÍA!

LOP!
EEP!
ZANG!

¡VIVA PICA!
¡VIVA PICA!

LO GRACIOSO ES QUE ES VERDAD.*
HA! HA! HA! HA!
HA! HA! HA! HA!
*IT'S FUNNY BECAUSE IT'S TRUE.

Dear Diary,
While everyone else enjoys the hospitality of our despotic host, I choose to explore Bosqueverde's natural splendor.

This is nature undisturbed by man or mini-mall.
AH.

I'll have to look this woodland friend up in "Little Ms. Know-it-all's Book of Creatures".

RARRRRRRR!

YAAAAAAH!
?
In fact, I think I'll go get that book right away.

OH, NO!

GENETICALLY-ALTERED FOOD!

STOP! ¡ALTO!
CUT IT OUT!

THINK ABOUT WHAT YOU'RE DOING! YOU'RE DESECRATING MOTHER NATURE'S PLANS AND RISKING A GENETIC HOLOCAUST WITH THESE SCIENTIFIC MOCKERIES OF THE EARTH'S BOUNTY!

SHE HAS SEEN THE BANANAS GIGANTES!
SHE CANNOT BE ALLOWED TO ESCAPE!

WELL...AH... ¡ADIÓS!

¡NIÑA IDIOTA!
GET HER!

WHEW! LOST THEM.
FOR A DEVELOPING NATION THIS PLACE IS PRETTY LAME.
WHERE'S THE CONSCIENCE OF BOSQUEVERDE?

SO, THERE'S **SOME** HOPE AFTER ALL.
¡VAMOS! ¡ÁNDALE!
THE PEOPLE'S REVOLUTIONARY PEOPLE'S ARMY OF BOSQUEVERDE
THIS IS A
SMOKE FREE JUNGLE
MEAN PEOPLE SUCK
FUR IS MURDER
AMERICAN POP STARS WELCOME

KLAK! SHAK!
OOP.
SNIK!
K-KLAK!!

LOOK, I'M ON **YOUR** SIDE. REALLY!
I **APPRECIATE** THAT YOU WANT TO STICK IT TO THE MAN.
MOVE ALONG, BLONDIE.

I AM COMANDANTE W.
DOUBLE-U?
ALL THE **GOOD** LETTERS WERE TAKEN.

WE FIGHT FOR FREEDOM AND THE RIGHT TO VOTE FOR ME. SO, YOU ARE **SIMPÁTICA** WITH OUR CAUSE.
AS LONG AS IT'S ABOUT JUSTICE FOR ALL LIVING THINGS.
SOMETHING LIKE THAT. THERE ARE **OTHER** AMERICANOS HERE AS WELL.

KRIS KRISTOFFERSON.
VIVA LA REVOLUCIÓN, MI AMIGA.

SHERYL CROW.
NICE TO SEE YOU.

ALEC BALDWIN.
I'VE **GOT** TO STOP SAYING I'LL LEAVE THE COUNTRY EVERY TIME SOMEONE I DON'T LIKE RUNS FOR OFFICE.

THE GUY WHO PLAYED URKEL.
WHAT CAN I **SAY**? IT'S A **GIG**.

I HATE TO **SAY** THIS, BUT EVEN FOR A GUERILLA LAIR THIS IS PRETTY LOW RENT.
TELL ME ABOUT IT. IF NOT FOR THE MONEY FROM TED TURNER, WE WOULD BE IN EVEN WORSE SHAPE.
AND EVEN **HE** MAKES DEMANDS OF US.

WHAT WE NEED ARE **FRESH** IDEAS FOR DISRUPTING GENERAL HIDALGO'S PUPPET STATE.
IDEAS THAT DO NOT REQUIRE MUCH **CASH** OUTLAY.
COMANDANTE, I MAY HAVE THE SOLUTION TO **ALL** YOUR PROBLEMS.
WATCH NCAA ACTION ON
TNT

BART?
BART?

BART!

BART, IT'S **ME**!
AYE CARUMBA!

WATCH YOUR LANGUAGE IN FRONT OF MY NIÑO!
OW!
SLAP!

WHAT'D I SAY?
HEY, WHERE'VE YOU **BEEN**, LIS'? **MOM** WAS LOOKING FOR YOU.
NO TIME FOR THAT. LISTEN **UP**, BART. THIS MAY BE THE OPPORTUNITY OF A **LIFETIME**.

LET ME GET THIS **STRAIGHT**...
YOU WANT ME TO HELP YOU PLAY MINDLESS PRANKS AND POSSIBLY DANGEROUS PRACTICAL JOKES TO DISRUPT THE STATUS QUO OF YOUR WHOLE **COUNTRY**?

JUST THINK OF GENERAL HIDALGO AS PRINCIPAL SKINNER.
TEMPTING... TEMPTING...

REVOLUTION FOR THE HELL OF IT?
SIGN ME UP!

!GENERAL!
THE PRESIDENT OF THE UNITED STATES IS ON THE PHONE!
I'LL TAKE IT ON LINE TWO.

SEÑOR PRESIDENTE, HOW MAY I ASSIST YOU?
I'M LOOKING FOR ONE OF MY AMBASSADORS.
ALLOW ME TO HELP.

HER NAME IS MARY COHEN.
I SHALL ASK FOR HER.
POR FAVOR. HAS ANY ONE SEEN MARY COHEN?

I AM LOOKING FOR A MARY COHEN. WILL SOMEONE FIND A MARY COHEN FOR ME?
WHAT IS SO HUMOROSO?
SNORT!
MARICON... GIGGLE.*
*MARICON=SISSY

HA! HA! HA! HA! HA! HA!
WHERE IS THIS MARY COHEN I SEEK?
HA! HA! HA! HA! HA! HA! HA! HA! HA!

THE PSYCHOLOGICAL PHASE OF MY ATTACK HAS BEGUN.
NOW WE GET SERIOUS.

"THIS WILL BE MY MASTERPIECE."
EL GENERAL IS A WIENER
EL GENERAL IS A WIENER
EL GENERAL IS A WIENER
EL GENERAL IS A WIENER
ZZZZZZZ

"AN ENTIRE CITY OF EXPLODING TOILETS."
AIEEEEEE!
SPLOOSH!
SPLOOSH!
SPLOOSH!
SPLOOSH!

"AN AUTHORITY FIGURE TO HUMILIATE."
HA!
HA!
HA!
HA!
HA!

"A BUNCH OF GOONS TO GOOF ON."
QUE?
EL BANGO
EL BANGO
EL BANGO

"AN ARMY OF WILLING ACCOMPLICES."
I'M WITH STUPIDO!

"PINCH ME, I'M DREAMING."
I DID NOT ORDER TWO HUNDRED PIZZAS!
ISN'T THIS 600 BLOODY COUP BOULEVARD?

YOU SAY YOU ARE WILLING TO TELL ME THE IDENTITY OF THIS VANDAL WHO PLAGUES MY EVERY WAKING MOMENT?
AND WHAT DO YOU WISH IN RETURN...

...SEÑOR SKINNER?
NOT A THING, GENERAL, SO LONG AS YOU KEEP HIM IN YOUR COUNTRY UNTIL HE'S EIGHTEEN.
The Springfield Shopper
BOSQUEVERDE PLAGUED BY PRANKSTER

THIS TOMFOOLERY HAS ALL THE EARMARKS OF ONE BART SIMPSON OF SPRINGFIELD, U.S.A.
The Springfield Shopper

SO, OUR GUESTS HAVE GONE FROM TOURIST TO TERRORIST.
I WANT THEM TO BE FOUND AND TO MEET WITH AN UNFORTUNATE AND HORRIFYING ACCIDENT!

MOM!
MOM!
WHAT IS IT, KIDS?

LISA GOT ME TO JOIN SOME REBEL FRIENDS OF HERS, AND NOW THE ARMY HAS ORDERS TO SHOOT TO KILL ME.
IT'S TRUE, MOM! BART MAY HAVE ACTUALLY OVER-ACHIEVED THIS TIME.

WELL, I GUESS WE'LL HAVE TO GET YOUR FATHER AND SEE ABOUT LEAVING.

EL CASINO GRANDE
YOU WIN AGAIN, SEÑOR SIMPSON.
I AM NEVER LEAVING THIS PLACE!

LOOK AT ALL THIS MOOLAH!
YOU HAVE WON EIGHTEEN MILLION BOSQUEVERDAN CHU-CHUS.
HOW MUCH IS IT IN AMERICAN?
I SHALL CALCULATE IT, SEÑOR.

HOMER, WE'RE ALL IN GREAT DANGER!
WE GOTTA LEAVE NOW, DAD!
WHAT? AND LEAVE A FORTUNE BEHIND?

IT IS SIX DOLLARS AND TWENTY-NINE CENTS IN YOUR DOLLARS, SEÑOR.
SEE?

THERE THEY ARE!
ALL BETTING IS CLOSED UNTIL THE EXECUTION IS OVER.
WE HAVE TO RUN, DAD!

MY FAMILY IS GOING TO BE MURDERED...AND ON FAJITAS NIGHT!
BLAM!
BLAM!

THE NORTEAMERICANOS ARE TO BE BUTCHERED BY OUR OPPRESSORS!
YES! THEY WILL MAKE A TELEVISION MOVIE ABOUT THIS!
THIS IS THE MOMENT WE HAVE WAITED FOR.
BY FEBRUARY SWEEPS WE COULD BE FREE!
WATCH NCAA ACTION ON
TNT

¡ALTO, GRINGOS!
YOU WILL STAND STILL TO BE SHOT, POR FAVOR.
WHUPPA!
WHUPPA!
EEP!

BRRRRRRRT!
IF WE GET GUNNED DOWN IN A HAIL OF HOT LEAD, YOU ARE IN BIG TROUBLE, BOY!
SORRY, HOMESLICE!

INTO THE JUNGLE!
WE CAN HIDE THERE!

WHERE'S FLANDERS' WEED-WHACKER WHEN WE NEED IT?
IT'S AT HOME IN OUR GARAGE.
STUPID FLANDERS! WHAT GOOD IS IT DOING US THERE?

STOP RIGHT THERE!
GAAAAAAAH!
TAKE THE BOY! HE DID IT!

GOOD AH-FTERNOON. I AM RAINIER WOLFCASTLE, CURRENTLY FILMING "MCBAIN XII: THE DAY AFTER THE LAST DAY ON EARTH."
WE NEED EX-TRAHS TO PLAY TERRIFIED AH-MERICAN HOSTAGES.
SHOW US TO OUR TRAILER, MR. WOLFCASTLE!

WELL, IT LOOKS LIKE WE'RE GOING HOME.
I CAN'T WAIT, MARGE. THIS IS THE WORST VACATION EVER. IT'S LIKE I'VE BEEN CURSED!

HEH
HEH
HEH
HEH
HEH

HEH
HEH HEH
QUIT THAT MANIACAL LAUGHTER, BARNEY.
IT'S CREEPIN' ME OUT.
HEH
HEH HEH
THE END

Beauty School HELLCATS

SPRINGFIELD DEPARTMENT OF MOTOR VEHICLES...

G'ON AN' TAKE MAH PITCHER, MISSY DMV LADY! I GOTS TO GET A LICENSE IF'N I WANTS T' DRIVE MAH TRACTOR TO CHURCH ON SUNDAY!

HOLD YOUR WATER, JETHRO. YOU CAN'T RUSH ART.

NOW, **SMILE**.

HIS LEF' SIDE GOTS A LOT MORE **TEETH**.

GAIL SIMONE	JOHN COSTANZA	TIM BAVINGTON	ART VILLANUEVA/RICK REESE	KAREN BATES	MATT GROENING
STORY	PENCILS	INKS	COLORS	LETTERS	DRIVING INSTRUCTOR

WHY, THESE HERE PITCHERS IS TOO PURTY FOR TA PUT ON A DUMB OL' LICENSE!
I...I FEELS SO UN-REPULSIVE!
LET'S GO HOME AN' COMMENCE TO SOME BABY-MAKIN' AFORE A BUG GETS STUCK IN YORE BEAUTIFUL HAIR, CLETUS!
DMV-SAT RELAY
DEE-DEET!
DEE-DEET!
DMV-1
COMMANDER! WE'RE GETTING A DMV-SATCOM REPORT OF A CLERK IN OUR SPRINGFIELD OFFICE--
SHE'S...SHE'S TAKING FLATTERING LICENSE PHOTOS, SIR!
BLAST!
GET ME HER OFFICE SUPERVISOR, NOW!
SOON...
?
MISS BOUVIER, WOULD YOU STEP INTO MY OFFICE FOR A MOMENT PLEASE?
UH, OH.

SELMA, DO YOU *LIKE* WORKING HERE?
OF COURSE NOT. I *HATE* IT HERE. IT'S *DEHUMANIZING* AND *SPIRIT-CRUSHING*.
GOOD, GOOD.

I'LL BE FRANK, SELMA. UP UNTIL RECENTLY, YOU'VE NEVER SHOWN AN *OUNCE* OF CREATIVITY, NOR HAVE YOU *EVER* PERFORMED YOUR WORK WITH THE SLIGHTEST ENTHUSIASM.
IN SHORT, YOU'VE BEEN A *PERFECT EMPLOYEE*.
SO, WHY NOT TAKE A NICE, *LONG* VACATION? FIND A WAY TO *RID* YOURSELF OF THESE..."*CREATIVE IMPULSES*."

PLEASE WAIT YOUR TURN TO BE FIRED! YOU ARE NUMBER:
41
BECAUSE IF YOU STILL *HAVE* THEM WHEN YOU COME BACK...I'M AFRAID YOU'LL HAVE TO TAKE A *NUMBER*.

HEY, WHERE ARE *YOU* GOING?
TO ENROLL IN BEAUTY SCHOOL, LIKE I'VE ALWAYS DREAMED!
HOT DOG! HANG ON, I'M COMING WITH YOU!
FAILED
OH, MAN, I *KNEW* I SHOULDN'T HAVE DRAWN THAT AWESOME HOT ROD ON MY TEST FORM!

WHAT ABOUT THE PEOPLE STILL IN LINE?
HEH. GOOD ONE. "WHAT ABOUT THE PEOPLE STILL IN LINE." HEH.
HEH. AHEH.

SOON...
PATTY, I CAN'T BELIEVE IT! I'M *FINALLY* GOING TO BEAUTY SCHOOL!
OUTDATED MAGAZINES AND UNLIMITED GOSSIP, *HERE WE COME!*
Mister Pierre's Academé of Beauty and Image (Formerly Pete's Budget Bowl Cuts)

TWO TO SIGN UP FOR CLASSES, PLEASE.
UH, WE DON'T ALLOW PETS...
I HAVE NO SENSE OF SMELL. THIS IS MY 'SMELLING-NOSE LIZARD,' JUB-JUB.
IT'S LIKE A SEEING-EYE DOG THAT DOESN'T LICK ITSELF.

WELL, OKAY...YOU'LL BE WITH THE OTHER NEW STUDENTS IN MR. PIERRE'S GROUP.
GOOD MORNING, LADIES. WELCOME TO HAIRSTYLING HELL!
GULP!

YOU WILL BE ISSUED ONE REGULATION PINK SMOCK. YOU WILL MASTER THE INTRICACIES OF PRECISION HAIRCUTTING, IF I HAVE TO BEAT IT INTO YOU!
THIS ISN'T "SUPERCUTS," LADIES. THIS IS MY WORLD.
AND TUCK IN THAT LIZARD!

DAY TWO...
WE'LL START WITH BASIC SHAMPOOING... THAT'S EXCELLENT WETTING TECHNIQUE, THERE, MISS PATTY.
MISS SELMA! WHAT IS YOUR MAJOR MALFUNCTION?
IT'S NOT MY FAULT! I CAN'T GET HIS HEAD IN THE SHAMPOO BOWL!

HELP! THIS WOMAN IS A MENACE TO THOSE WITH UNUSUAL FOLLICLE ORNAMENTATION!

DAY FOURTEEN...
MISS SELMA! THIS HAIR IS NEITHER BOUNCING NOR BEHAVING!
I'M ASHAMED TO SAY THAT ONE OF MY TRAINEES COMMITTED THIS ASYMMETRICAL ATROCITY!

DAY THIRTY-SEVEN...
SELMA! THAT'S NOT HAIRSPRAY--IT'S PURE PEROXIDE!
DUDE, MY EYES ARE LIKE TOTALLY LIQUEFYING!

DAY SIXTY-FIVE...
YOU'RE NEVER GOING TO PASS THE PRACTICAL EXAM AT THIS RATE, BOUVIER! YOU SHOULD DROP OUT IMMEDIATELY!
SOB!
I GOT NO PLACE ELSE TO GO!

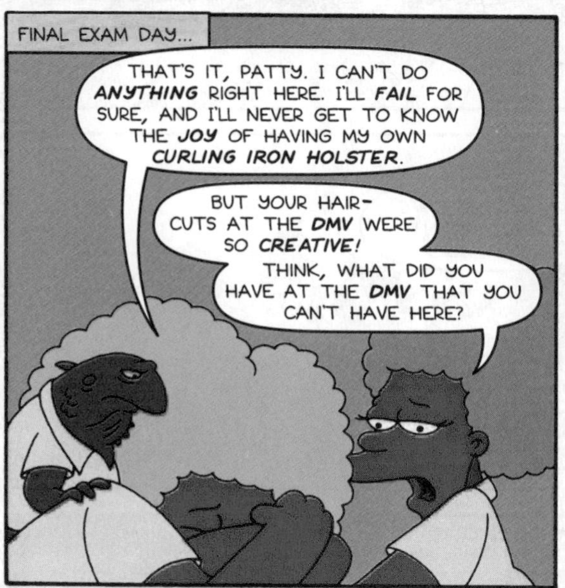
FINAL EXAM DAY...
THAT'S IT, PATTY. I CAN'T DO ANYTHING RIGHT HERE. I'LL FAIL FOR SURE, AND I'LL NEVER GET TO KNOW THE JOY OF HAVING MY OWN CURLING IRON HOLSTER.
BUT YOUR HAIR-CUTS AT THE DMV WERE SO CREATIVE!
THINK, WHAT DID YOU HAVE AT THE DMV THAT YOU CAN'T HAVE HERE?

NICOTINE, TAR AND OTHER TOXINS!!
NO TIME TO UNWRAP, JUST LIGHT THE WHOLE PACK!

AH, THAT'S THE STUFF!
NOW, LET ME AT THEM SCALPS! THEY NEED SOME SELMA-GINATION!

YOU'RE LATE, LADIES! YOUR FINAL EXAM VOLUNTEERS ARE WAITING!
NOW GO, BOTH OF YOU! GO AND MAKE MR. PIERRE PROUD! SNIFF!

CONGRATULATIONS, SELMA. YOU'VE **EARNED** THIS DIPLOMA.
I...I NEVER WOULDA MADE IT IF NOT FOR YOU.
ARE YOU **SEEING** ANYONE CURRENTLY BY CHANCE?
:CHOKE: GET THE HELL OUT OF HERE.

I'M SO PROUD OF YOU BOTH! WHAT **NEXT**? ARE YOU GOING TO **OPEN A SALON**?
NO, MY DREAM CAME TRUE ALREADY. IT'S BACK TO THE **DMV** FOR US! THEY PROBABLY HAVE A LINE OF CUSTOMERS OUT THE DOOR BY NOW.
OH YEAH. WE'D BETTER HURRY. AHEH. HEH.
HEH. AHEH, HEH!
NEXT: LIZARD MAKEOVERS!

SET A COURSE FOR DIVORCE!

SIMPSONS COMICS

#66

US $2.50
CAN $3.50

HOMER'S LUV BOAT

PLUS: A TOP SECRET TOUR OF THE GLOBEX CORPORATION WITH HANK SCORPIO!

CRUISIN' for a BRUISIN'

MY WIFE IS ***DEAD?!!***

IAN BOOTHBY SCRIPT ***PHIL ORTIZ*** PENCILS ***PHYLLIS NOVIN*** INKS ***KAREN BATES*** LETTERS

ART VILLANUEVA/RICK REESE COLORS ***BILL MORRISON*** EDITOR ***MATT GROENING*** O CAPTAIN, MY CAPTAIN

NO, I KEEP TELLING YOU! IT'S **MY** WIFE THAT PASSED AWAY!
WHICH IS WHY I'M TRYING TO GIVE YOU OUR TICKETS TO A ***ROMANTIC COUPLES CRUISE*** WE BOOKED A YEAR AGO.

DID YOU SAY A ***CRUISE***?
ZZIP!

WELL, I'D LIKE TO GO, FLANDERS, BUT I'M ***TERRIFIED OF WATER***.
THANK YOU, NED. WE'D BE HAPPY TO TAKE YOUR TICKETS.
SWIPE!

BUT MARGE.
OH, HOMER. JUST CALL UP DR. HIBBERT AND HAVE HIM CURE YOUR ***RABIES!***
AND GET RID OF THAT RACCOON!

SOB! GOODBYE, MR. NIBBLES!

THREE DAYS AND SEVERAL PAINFUL INJECTIONS LATER...
CAPTAIN McCALLISTER'S
CRUISING ADVENTURES!
NOT ASSOCIATED WITH THE AL PACINO FILM 'CRUISING'
WELCOME ABOARD YE' LANDLUBBIN' LOVEBIRDS!
CHECK IT OUT, MARGE! THE BARNACLES SMELL LIKE POTPOURRI!
NOW THAT'S CLASS!

OH, HOMER, LOOK AT THE POOL.
YAWN

OOOH, A TRAINED DOLPHIN!
EH!

AND IT'S SERVING DRINKS.
OUT OF MY WAY!
FINALLY, AN ANIMAL THAT DOES SOMETHING USEFUL BESIDES TASTE GOOD!

ARE YOU THIRSTY, FELLA?
HEY, MARGE! HE WANTS A **BEER,** TOO!

NOOOOOOOOO!

SKIPPER'S **ON THE WAGON!** HE WAS JUST TWO DAYS AWAY FROM HIS SIX MONTH AA CHIP!

SO IS SKIPPER A HAPPY DRUNK OR AN ANGRY DRUNK?

SQUEEEE!!
AAAAAAAH!

LATER...
NOT SO SMART NOW ARE YA', MR. DOLPHIN?
AAAR! YE BE **BANNED** FROM ALL MY CRUISES IN THE FUTURE!

FINE! I'LL SHOW YOU! I'LL JUST START MY OWN CRUISE SHIP BUSINESS!
HRRMMM.

MARGE, WHAT'S WITH THE "HRRMMM"?
OH, HOMER. 95% OF **NEW BUSINESSES** IN SPRINGFIELD FAIL IN THE FIRST YEAR. AND 85% OF THOSE ARE STARTED BY **YOU**.

MARGE, THIS ISN'T LIKE THE SNOW PLOW, INTERNET, ELEPHANT RIDE, COUNTRY MUSIC MANAGEMENT, GREASE RECYCLING, BODYGUARDING, RACEHORSE OWNING, LOVE POTION, CHIROPRACTOR, BEER BARONING OR DAYCARE BUSINESSES.
THIS'LL BE DIFFERENT!

YOU WANT **MORE TIME** OFF WORK?
SPRINGFIELD NUCLEAR POWER PLANT

FRANKLY, SIMPSON, I'M NOT EVEN SURE YOU **WORK** HERE ANY MORE.
I STILL GET A **PAY-CHECK**.

TAKING YOU OFF PAYROLL WOULD MEAN REPLACING ALL THE ACCOUNTING DEPARTMENT'S **ABACUSES**.
I WISH MR. BURNS WOULD LET US USE COMPUTERS.

PISH TOSH! COMPUTERS ARE JUST A ***FAD,*** SMITHERS. LIKE THE LINDSEY HOP AND POLIO.
MR. BURNS!
HELLO, SIR!

NO TIME TO TALK TO THE ***DRONE,*** SMITHERS. CONVEY MY GREETING TO HIM LATER. I NEED YOU TO TAKE ***MY YACHT*** TO THE DUMP.
I STILL CAN'T GET THE SMELL OUT FROM THE TIME SIMON LEBON OWNED IT.

I'LL TAKE THE SHIP TO THE DUMP FOR YOU, MR. SMITHERS.
GOOD MAN, SIMPSON. YOU MIGHT ***EARN*** YOUR PAYCHECK THIS WEEK AFTER ALL.

A WEEK LATER...
BEHOLD! A SHIP SO ***MIGHTY*** THAT GOD HIMSELF COULDN'T ***SINK IT!***
~~GONE FISSION~~
HOMER'S SUPER BOAT

HEY, HOMER! WHERE DO YOU WANT THIS ICE FOR THE BAR DRINKS?

KERASH!

THE NEXT WEEK...
I WOULD LIKE TO *RETRACT* MY EARLIER STATEMENT ABOUT GOD AND HIS SHIP-SINKING ABILITIES. I'D ALSO LIKE TO TAKE THIS TIME TO *PRAISE* BUDDHA, ALLAH, AND, TO A LESSER EXTENT, RA!
GONE FISSION
HOMER'S SUPER BOAT

GIVE A GOOD WORD TO THE MAN UPSTAIRS FOR US, WOULD YOU, REVEREND?
WILL DO!

WELCOME ABOARD HOMER'S *SUPERBOAT CRUISELINE OF LOVE!*
SMILES EVERYONE! SMILES!

SO WHO ARE THESE COUPLES, HOMER?
WHAT DO YOU MEAN, BOY? YOU **KNOW** EVERYBODY.

MAYBE, I JUST LIKE HEARING EXPOSITION-STYLE CHARACTER DESCRIPTIONS, OKAY?
FINE, KNOCK YOURSELF OUT!

THERE'S PRINCIPAL SKINNER AND YOUR TEACHER MRS. KRABAPPEL.
LOOKS LIKE HE'S BROUGHT HIS WORK WITH HIM, AND SHE'S NOT ***TOO HAPPY*** ABOUT IT.

THE NEWLY-DIVORCED LUANN VAN HOUTEN AND HER BOYFRIEND PYRO...

...AND THERE'S HER EX-HUSBAND, KIRK VAN HOUTEN, WHO'S WITH HIS ***NEW GIRLFRIEND,*** TENILLE.
WHERE'S SHE?
I CAN HEAR YOU, AND SHE'S RUNNING A BIT LATE, OKAY?

THERE'S APU AND MANJULA, RECENTLY BLESSED WITH ***OCTUPLETS***.
HEY, HOMER, IMAGINE IF I WAS AN OCTUPLET. WOULDN'T THAT BE ***COOL***?
SHUDDER. THAT THOUGHT IS GONNA TAKE A LOT OF BEER TO WASH AWAY.

THE MILLIONAIRE AND HIS WIFE.

HOW COME BART DOESN'T HAVE TO SWAB THE DECKS?
I CALLED "NO SWABBING" FIRST.
NOTHING I CAN DO, LISA. IT'S THE LAW OF THE SEA.
YOU KNOW, HOMER, I WAS AGAINST THIS AT FIRST, BUT BEING OUT HERE IN THE SEA AIR IS FUN.

OH, MARGE, I CAN ALWAYS COUNT ON YOU...
...TO FOLD LIKE A HOUSE OF CARDS.

YOU KNOW YOU SAID THAT SECOND SENTENCE OUT LOUD. RIGHT, DAD?

D'OH!

WILL YOU STOP UPDATING STUDENTS' PERMANENT RECORDS, SEYMOUR? WE'RE HERE TO RELAX TOGETHER!

THE LAST TIME I RELAXED I ENDED UP IN A P.O.W CAMP EATING DUNG BEETLES.
ALWAYS WITH THE DUNG BEETLES.
AT LEAST TAKE OFF YOUR SUIT AND TIE.

FOR THE LAST TIME, NO!

HMMMF!

WELL, THAT'S GOING ON HER PERMANENT RECORD.

HOMER, I THINK PRINCIPAL SKINNER AND MRS. KRABAPPEL'S RELATIONSHIP IS IN TROUBLE.
RELAX, MARGE, I'VE SEEN EVERY EPISODE OF "THE LOVE BOAT" AND "THE NEW LOVE BOAT."

ALL A TROUBLED RELATIONSHIP NEEDS IS A ZANY MISUNDER-STANDING.
BUT...
OH, FIRST MATE BART?

SOON...
EDNA IS HAVING AN AFFAIR WITH PYRO?!!
TO THE BEST OF MY KNOWLEDGE, YES.

THAT NIGHT...
WHERE'S YOUR GIRLFRIEND, MR. VAN HOUTEN?
UH...SHE'S SEA SICK.
WELCOME TO THE CAPTAIN'S TABLE. RELAX, EAT AND LET THE LOVE VIBES FLOW.

PASS THE PEAS?
I GUESS HE'D KNOW ABOUT MAKING PASSES. RIGHT, EDNA?

CAN I HAVE THE HAM THEN?
WHAT?

WHY DON'T YOU CHEW ON THIS KNUCKLE SANDWICH, HOMEWRECKER!
SOCK!

WHAM!
JUST IGNORE THEM! THEY'RE JUST HAVING A BOUT OF OCEAN MADNESS. THEY'LL GET THEIR SEA BRAINS SOON!
GO ABOUT YOUR LOVE TALK!

OH, APU, IT'S SO NICE TO SPEND TIME BY OURSELVES.
YES, WE FINALLY HAVE A CHANCE TO TALK TO EACH OTHER ABOUT SOMETHING OTHER THAN THE CHILDREN.

SO...
SO...

HOW'S THE KWIK-E-MART?
FINE, FINE. WITH NELSON GETTING HIS TONSILS OUT SHOPLIFTING IS DOWN 30%.

SWEET VISHNU! WE HAVE NOTHING TO SAY TO EACH OTHER ANYMORE!

MARRIAGE AND KIDS HAVE DRIED UP THE OLD CONVERSATION WELL, 'EH?
HERE'S A TOPIC. AT YOUR WEDDING, SINCE REVEREND LOVEJOY DIDN'T KNOW MUCH ABOUT YOUR CULTURE, ODDS ARE YOU'RE NOT REALLY MARRIED.

GASP!

MANJULA, NO! **COME BACK!**

THAT GOT THE **OLD PASSION** BACK.

PYRO! I ATE MY ENTIRE DINNER **ALONE**. YOU PROMISED YOU WOULDN'T LET YOUR **LOVE OF BATTLE** INTERFERE WITH OUR LOVE.
THIS HAS NOTHING TO DO WITH MY "AMERICAN GLADIATOR" TRAINING. I...

MAYBE WHEN YOU'RE FINISHED PLAYING WITH **YOUR FRIEND,** YOU'LL HAVE TIME FOR ME.

YOU ONLY MARRIED ME FOR **MY MONEY**!

WELL, YOU ONLY MARRIED **ME** FOR **MY** MONEY!

YEP, IT'S ALL GOING **ACCORDING TO PLAN**.
BUT DARLING I...
HRMMPH!
MOTHER WAS RIGHT, I SHOULD HAVE MARRIED THAT BILLIONAIRE!
WELL, I SHOULD HAVE MARRIED THAT TRILLIONAIRE!
NOW SEE HERE...
DON'T "SEE HERE" ME!

YOU KNOW, HOMER, MAYBE YOU SHOULD SPEND LESS TIME **MATCHMAKING** AND MORE TIME ACTUALLY **STEERING THE SHIP**.
!!
THERE'S A STEERING WHEEL?

THAT'S IT! WE'RE **LOST AT SEA** AND DESTROYING EVERYONE'S RELATIONSHIPS.
I'M TAKING OVER!

LATER...
HAVE YOU THOUGHT ABOUT WHAT YOU'VE DONE? ARE YOU READY TO COME OUT OF *THE BRIG*?
MUTINY.
MUTINY.
I WILL NOT COMMIT MUTINY.
I WILL NOT COMMIT MUTINY.
I WILL NOT COMMIT MUTINY.
I WILL NOT COMMIT MUTINY.
I WILL NOT COMMIT
I WILL NOT COMMIT
I WILL NOT COM
YES'M.

WE STILL LOST?
LISA IS NAVIGATING, AND HOMER'S GETTING THE HANG OF THE WHEEL.

WATCH IT! YOU ALMOST HIT US!
SORRY! MY BAD!
MON DIEU!
IDIOT!

WHERE'S YOUR *GIRLFRIEND,* KIRK?
UH...SHE HAD TO WRITE A LETTER TO HER MOTHER.
SUUUURE SHE DID.

YOU TWO HAVE TO MAKE UP!
NO, WE DON'T.
WE'RE THROUGH!

WE'RE NOT MARRIED.
BUT A MARRIED COUPLE HAS TO MAKE UP AFTER AN ARGUMENT!

YOU ARE NOW! I'M THE CAPTAIN, AND I CAN MARRY WHO-EVER I WANT!
THAT'S THE MOST RIDICULOUS...

UH... DAD?

NOT NOW, LISA, DADDY'S PLAYING GOD.
BUT DAD...

...PIRATES!
YIPES!!!

OKAY, OKAY DON'T PANIC. WE'LL JUST GIVE THEM THE MILLIONAIRE'S MONEY, AND THEY'LL LEAVE US ALONE!

BUT WE DON'T HAVE ANY REAL MONEY!
WE'RE SOB DOT COM MILLIONAIRES!

PYRO! YOU CAN HELP US FIGHT THEM!
WHAT'S THE POINT? WITHOUT LOVE MY FIGHTING SPIRIT IS GONE!

WHAT DO YOU MEAN? YOU'VE GOT THE LOVE OF TWO WOMEN!
LUANN AND EDNA!

EDNA?
WHAT ARE YOU TALKING ABOUT? I LOVE YOU, NOT PYRO!
THEN YOU'RE NOT HAVING AN AFFAIR?

NO!
WELL GIVE ME A D- IN CONDUCT AND AN INCOMPLETE IN COMMON SENSE. I LOVE YOU TOO, EDNA.

DIVORCE US, HOMER.
DONE!
WHEW!

SO THAT'S WHY YOU WERE FIGHTING HIM? I'M SORRY FOR SNAPPING AT YOU. DARN THOSE WINE SPRITZERS. THEY TURN ME INTO A BEAST.
YOUR PASSION REMINDED ME WHY I FELL FOR YOU, LUANN VAN HOUTEN!

WELL, ALL THIS MAKING UP IS WELL AND GOOD FOR THE REST OF YOU, BUT WE ARE STILL NOT MAN AND WIFE, POSSIBLY.
AND THERE IS NOTHING ANY OF YOU CAN DO TO CHANGE THAT!

I'M CAPTAIN. YOU'RE MARRIED.
WELL, I CERTAINLY SET MYSELF UP FOR THAT!

I LOVE YOU, WIFE.
AND I YOU, HUSBAND.

AH...HAVE YOU ALL FORGOTTEN ABOUT THE PIRATES?

OH YOU'RE JUST BITTER BECAUSE YOUR GIRLFRIEND DOESN'T REALLY EXIST.
OH, YEAH. WELL, MAYBE YOUR BOYFRIEND DOESN'T EXIST, EITHER!

I'M RIGHT HERE.
YOU'VE WON THIS ROUND, LUANN!

ABANDON SHIP OR FACE OUR ***BOOTY CALL!***

ARE WE GOING TO LET PIRATES ***THREATEN*** THE ONES WE LOVE?
NO!

THEN LET'S GET THEM!
AAAAAR! UH...CAN WE TALK ABOUT THIS?

POW!
GAAAR!

THESE AREN'T PIRATES AT ALL! THEY'RE JUST ***CARD-BOARD CUTOUTS!***
AND ***THIS DOLPHIN*** WAS STEERING THE SHIP!

WAIT A MINUTE! THIS PIRATE IS REALLY...
YANK!

CAPTAIN MCCALLISTER!
AAAR! I JUST WANTED TO RUIN YER' CRUISE LIKE YOU RUINED MINE. AND I WOULD HAVE GOTTEN AWAY WITH IT, TOO...
...IF I WERE SMARTER.

OH, KIRK! DID I MISS ANYTHING?
YOUR GIRL-FRIEND IS REAL?!
AND REAL HOT! RRRRRROWL!

YEAH! SHE'S REAL! SO THERE!
CAPTAIN? IS THAT YOU?
TENILLE?

WHAT THE...?
SHE'S MY DARLING WIFE I THOUGHT LOST AT SEA YEARS AGO!

WELL, I DID MEET HER THROUGH A LOST AT SEA DATING SERVICE.

SO ASIDE FROM KIRK, EVERY-ONE'S HAPPY AND IN LOVE!
I'M THE BEST CRUISE GUY EVER!

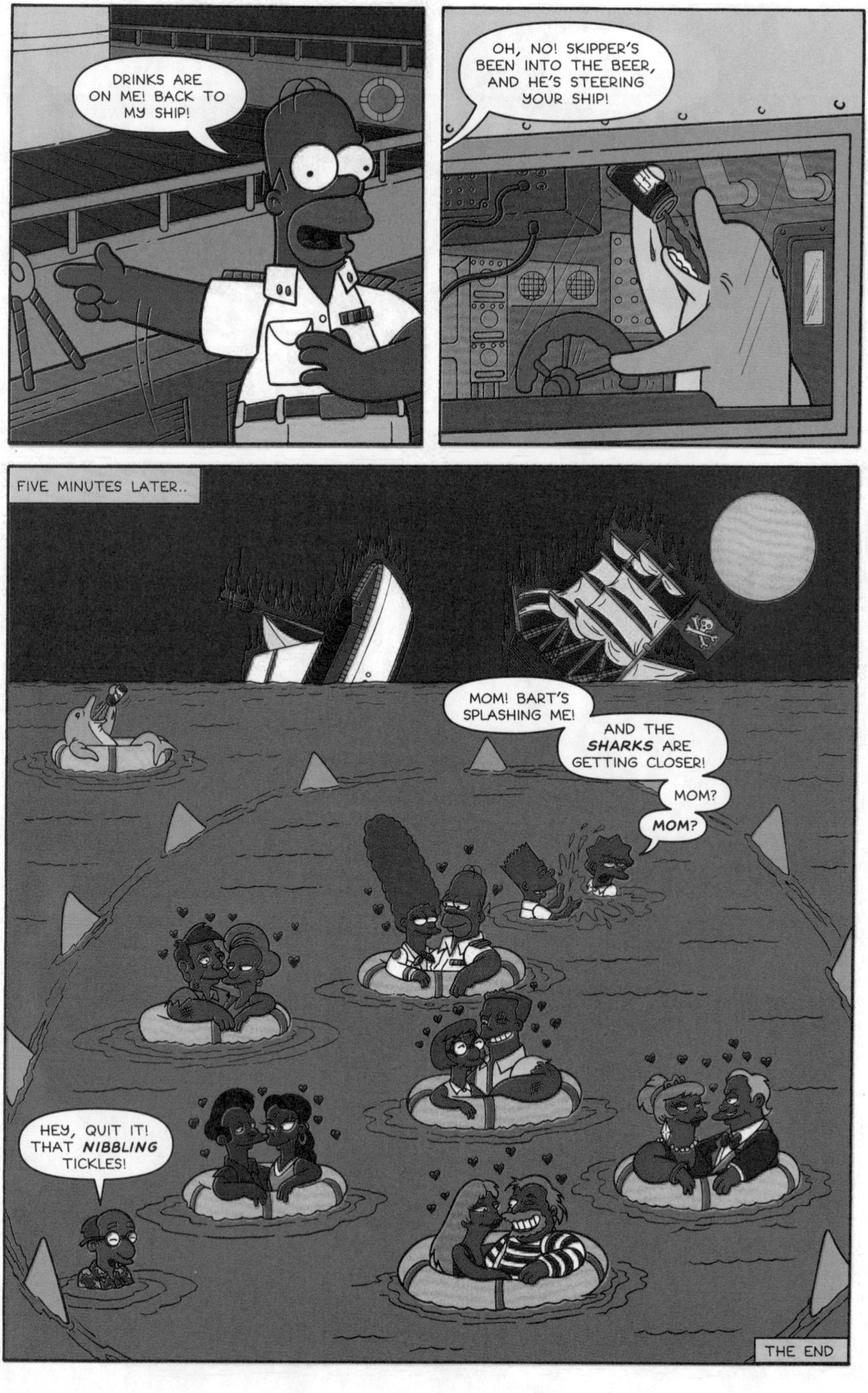

FIVE MINUTES LATER..

MOM! BART'S SPLASHING ME!

AND THE **SHARKS** ARE GETTING CLOSER!

MOM?

MOM?

HEY, QUIT IT! THAT **NIBBLING** TICKLES!

THE END

OH, IT'S **YOU**! AND YOU'RE **EARLY**!
LISTEN, I APPRECIATE THE EFFORT, BUT WE DON'T PAY MUCH ATTENTION TO OL' **MR. TIMECLOCK** HERE. YOU KNOW WHAT I MEAN?
WORLD'S GREATEST TYRANT

NOPE, IT'S **PEOPLE** THAT COUNT, AND JUST BY LOOKING AT YOU, I CAN TELL YOU'RE DEFINITELY **PEOPLE**.
HEY, CAN I GET YOU ANYTHING?

OH, YOU **GOTTA** TRY THESE **SOY-POPS**. THESE ARE GONNA BE **HUGE** IN THE HEALTH SNACK MARKET... THEY'RE **DELICIOUS**!
I THINK I'LL HAVE ONE MYSELF!

OKAY, I'LL BE VERY HONEST WITH YOU. THAT WASN'T DELICIOUS AT ALL. THE BOYS IN R&D CAN BUILD A **LASER DEATH-TRAP** YOU WOULDN'T BELIEVE, BUT THEY CAN'T ENGINEER A DECENT **PINEAPPLE-FLAVORED SOY-POP**, BLESS THEIR HEARTS!
GLOBE

LISTEN, I'VE GOT A GOOD FEELING ABOUT YOU. JUST LET ME ASK, FOR THE **RECORD**...

...SO YOU WANT TO WORK FOR GLOBEX, HUH?

GAIL SIMONE STORY · OSCAR GONZALEZ LOYO PENCILS · STEVE STEERE, JR. INKS · ART VILLANUEVA COLORS · KAREN BATES LETTERS · BILL MORRISON EDITOR · MATT GROENING MODEL EMPLOYEE

LOOK OUT! HE'S GOING ON ANOTHER MURDEROUS RAMPAGE!
I WEEL KEEL YOU, AMERICAN PEEG!

HA! HO! HO! HA! HO!
KIDDING! OH, BOY, WE HAVE A LOT OF FUN AROUND HERE, DON'T WE?
OH, C'EST BON! YOU TOTALLY FELL FOR EET, MON AMI!

...AND NOW, WE KEEL HEEM FOR TRUE!
NO, NO, NO!

I KEEL HEEM! I MAKE OF HEEM A DINNER FOR MY TRAINED GIANT WEASEL!
HEY, WHY DON'T WE JUST MOVE ALONG, HUH? WHATTYA SAY, SOUND GOOD? OKAY!

I WANT TO APOLOGIZE FOR THAT. SEE, HE'S GOT THIS TRAINED GIANT WEASEL, AND, WELL, HE'S ALWAYS TRYING TO SHOW IT OFF, YOU KNOW?
EXIT
IT'S KINDA CUTE WHEN YOU THINK ABOUT IT, HUH?

HEY, HEY! WHOA! WHERE YA GOIN'?
EXIT

OKAY, IT'S NOT CUTE. I ADMIT IT.
EXIT
SNAP!
NO POINT IN DENYING IT. SCARFACE HAS A BIT OF A HOMICIDAL IMPULSE PROBLEM, BUT HE'S A GOOD MAN, AND DARN IT, HE KNOWS HOW TO TRAIN A GIANT WEASEL!

LOOK, I CAN SEE YOU'RE A BIT CONCERNED ABOUT COMING TO WORK FOR ME, RIGHT?
WORRIED ABOUT GOING TO PRISON, I BET. WELL, LEMME SHOW YOU SOMETHING.
MULTI-MEDIA ROOM

YESTERDAY'S GLOBEX
STOCK MARKET TAMPERING
INDUSTRIAL SABOTAGE
INTERNATIONAL TERRORISM
ILLEGAL ARMS TRADING
COMIC BOOK COUNTERFEITING
TREASON
MILITARY ESPIONAGE
HABITUAL NAPSTER USAGE
GAME-SHOW FIXING
NOW, IT'S TRUE THAT IN THE PAST, MY COMPANY HAS BEEN INVOLVED IN SOME QUESTIONABLE VENTURES.

BUT, SEE, TODAY'S GLOBEX IS...
HEY, WHAT'S SO FUNNY?
TODAY'S GLOBEX!
HEALTH-FOOD MARKETING
NOVELTY SINGING FISH PRODUCTION
OSMOND SOUND-ALIKE RECORDING
BULK HYMNAL DISTRIBUTION
MAIL-ORDER WEDDING APPAREL
GLOBUL DOMINASHUN!
HA! HA! HA!
HAR! HAR!

"GLOBUL DOMINA..."
WHAT THE HEY?
TODAY'S GLOBEX!
HEALTH-FOOD MARKETING
NOVELTY SINGING FISH PRODUCTION
OSMOND SOUND-ALIKE RECORDING
BULK HYMNAL DISTRIBUTION
MAIL-ORDER WEDDING APPAREL
GLOBUL DOMINASHUN!

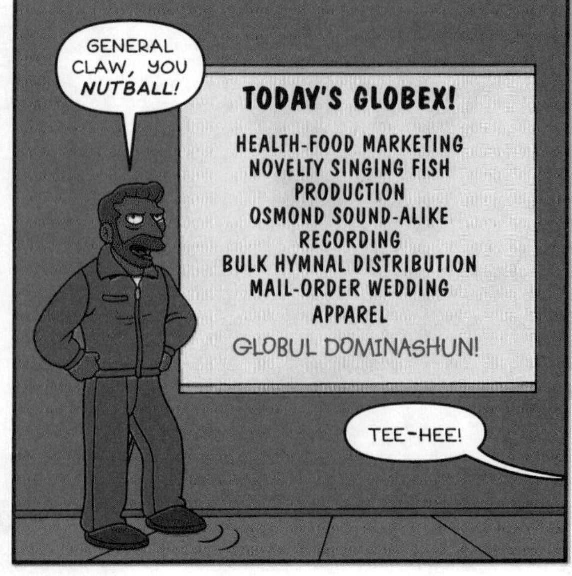
GENERAL CLAW, YOU NUTBALL!
TODAY'S GLOBEX!
HEALTH-FOOD MARKETING
NOVELTY SINGING FISH PRODUCTION
OSMOND SOUND-ALIKE RECORDING
BULK HYMNAL DISTRIBUTION
MAIL-ORDER WEDDING APPAREL
GLOBUL DOMINASHUN!
TEE-HEE!

THERE YOU ARE, SCORPIO! I'M HERE TO PUT AN END TO YOUR REIGN OF TERROR ONCE AND FOR ALL!
RRIIP!
OH, GREAT. AGENT JAMES BONT, AGAIN! JUST AS I'M INTERVIEWING OUR NEW JOB APPLICANT!

NOW, EXPLAIN THIS TO ME, GENERAL CLAW. DID YOU TIE HIM UP OVER THE PIT OF ALLIGATORS, LIKE I ASKED, WITH JUST A SMALL CANDLE...
...TO BURN SLOWLY THROUGH THE ROPE-- YES, I DID, MASTER, JUST AS YOU SAID!

WELL, THIS IS A FINE HOW-DO-YOU-DO!
HIS CONTINUED EXISTENCE FILLS ME WITH SHAME, MASTER!
BAM!
POW!
BASH!

HEY, NOW, ENOUGH WITH THAT "MASTER" TALK! THERE'S NO "TEAM" IN MASTER!
ACTUALLY, IF YOU RE-ARRANGE THE LETTERS AND REMOVE THE "R" AND THE "S"...
NOW WE'RE TALKIN'!

OKAY, I CONFESS, WE STILL DABBLE IN HOLDING THE WORLD HOSTAGE, JUST A BIT, BUT YOU'LL BARELY NOTICE IT.
IT'S A VERY COMPETITIVE FIELD!

I'M GONNA LEVEL WITH YOU, I'M BEING TOTALLY REAL HERE. WE WANT YOU HERE AT GLOBEX. CLAW, TELL HIM ABOUT THE CAFETERIA.
TUESDAY IS FIESTA DAY, WITH A FULL SALSA BAR!
I'M COMING FOR YOU, SCORPIO!

FULL USE OF THE COMPANY SAUNA!
COMPREHENSIVE MEDICAL AND DENTAL PLANS...
KEEL HEEM, MY PRECIOUS!!

HSSSSSSSSSS!!!!
COME ON, IT'LL BE FUN!
DO YOU LIKE SOFTBALL? YOU CAN PITCH FOR THE COMPANY TEAM!

WHAT? YOU WANT PROFIT-SHARING AND A COMPANY CAR?
WELL, I MUST SAY... I FIND THAT KIND OF GREED A LITTLE DISAPPOINTING!

HEY, SCARFACE! CAN YOU COME OVER HERE A MINUTE? WE HAVE A CONTRACT TO NEGOTIATE! OH, AND BRING YOUR WEASEL!
♫ I'M ♫ COMEENG!
HSSSSSSSSSS!!!!

THE
GLOBEX
CORPORATION
WE DOMINATE BECAUSE WE CARE!

Dr. Nick Riviera IN

CRIME FAMILY PRACTICE

HI, EVERYBODY!

HI, DR. NICK!

DAN FYBEL STORY · **OSCAR GONZALEZ LOYO** PENCILS · **MIKE ROTE** INKS · **CHRIS UNGAR** COLORS · **KAREN BATES** LETTERS · **MATT GROENING** DOC HOLLYWOOD

MY INCREDIBLY HIGH FEE WILL MAKE HIM FORGET HIS CERTAIN DEATH. DID I JUST SAY THAT ON THE AIR?
YOU EVER BURP AND SNEEZE AT THE SAME TIME? NOW, WOULD THAT BE A "SNURP" OR A "BNEEZE"? THE FUNNY THING ABOUT SNEEZING IS--
LINE TWO, I AM HERE TO MAKE YOU HEALTHY!

AN HOUR LATER...
WHAT A WONDERFUL FEELING TO HELP PEOPLE. OKAY, SEE YOU AGAIN WHEN MY APPOINTMENT BOOK LOOKS SKINNY!
THAT REMINDS ME OF THE TIME MY BUDDY, EARL, THE ONE WITH THE TURTLES--
GOODBYE, MR. RADIO MAN!

NOW WHERE DID I PARK MY WHEEL THINGY?

OH, HERE SHE IS!

NAB!

HELLO, DR. NICK.

ULP...HELLO, EVERYBODY.

I'LL CUT TO THE CANNOLI. YOU NEED NEW PATIENTS AND MY "FAMILY" NEEDS A NEW DOCTOR.
YOU'RE IN LUCK. I CAN MAYBE SQUEEZE YOU IN, SAY...FEBRUARY?
OR PERHAPS, SAY...RIGHT NOW?!

SOON...
I GOT YOUR CUSTOMERS RIGHT HERE, PALLY!
DR. NICK
BRIBERY ILLUSTRATED
EXTORTION DIGEST

WOULD YOU MIND KINDLY REMOVING THESE SHOES FOR ME? THEY'RE NOT MY SIZE, AND FRANKLY, I'M NOT SO FOND OF THE STYLE.
NURSE, MY JACKHAMMER! NEXT!

I WAS HOLDING A DOOR OPEN FOR A DEAR OLD LADY. IT WAS AN ESPECIALLY HEAVY DOOR.

LATER...
BOY, OH BOY. I NEVER WORK THIS MANY MINUTES IN A ROW. TIME FOR A NAP.

DR. NICK. PERHAPS YOU COULD BE OF ASSISTANCE.

HOLY HEMOGLOBIN, WHAT HAPPENED TO YOU?
OH THIS? YOU KNOW HOW PLAYFUL POLICE DOGS CAN GET SOMETIMES.
GRRR
GRRR

ALL THAT RED STUFF...OH, I'M STARTING TO FEEL A LITTLE WOOZY.
DR. NICK, I SUGGEST YOU QUICKLY GET OVER YOUR SQUEAMISHNESS, OR YOU WILL BE PERFORMING EMERGENCY SURGERY TO REMOVE MY BRUNO MAGLI SHOE FROM THE CRACK OF YOUR--
GRRR

OKAY, ALL RIGHT, LET ME THINK BACK TO MY DAYS OF ARDUOUS STUDY AT THE MEDICAL SCHOOL...
GRRR
GRRR
GRRR

"I MUST HAVE LEARNED SOMETHING ABOUT DOGS..."
HAIR OF THE DOG...

NO, THAT'S NOT IT.
EXCUSE ME, DR. NICK?
GRRR
GRRR
GRRR

...THEN THE COURSE DOGLEGS TO THE LEFT AFTER THAT SAND TRAP.
WILL ANY OF THIS BE ON THE BIOMETRY TEST, PROFESSOR?

NOPE. THAT DOESN'T SEEM TO HELP EITHER.
HEY, DOC...
GRRR
GRRR
GRRR

IT'S A DOG EAT DOG WORLD OUT THERE, RIVIERA.
YES! ANOTHER PASSING GRADE! THAT'S TWO IN A ROW!
A
D

"DOG EAT DOG..." THAT'S IT! HERE ARE SOME HOT DOGS TO SNACK ON, POOCHIES!

CHOMP!
CHOMP!
CHOMP!
NOW LOTS OF BANDAGES AND HAPPY PILLS FOR YOU, MR. SIR.

THANKS, DR. NICK. YOU'RE A LIFESAVER. JUST ONE LAST QUESTION BEFORE I DEPART. WHAT HAPPENS WHEN THOSE MUTTS POLISH OFF THE HOT DOGS?

NYAH!

GRRRRRR!

HOORAY! NOW I CAN SUE THE POLICE AND MAKE THEM GIVE BACK MY DOCTOR'S LICENSE!
GOODBYE, EVERYBODY!
GRRR
GRRR
GRRR
THE END

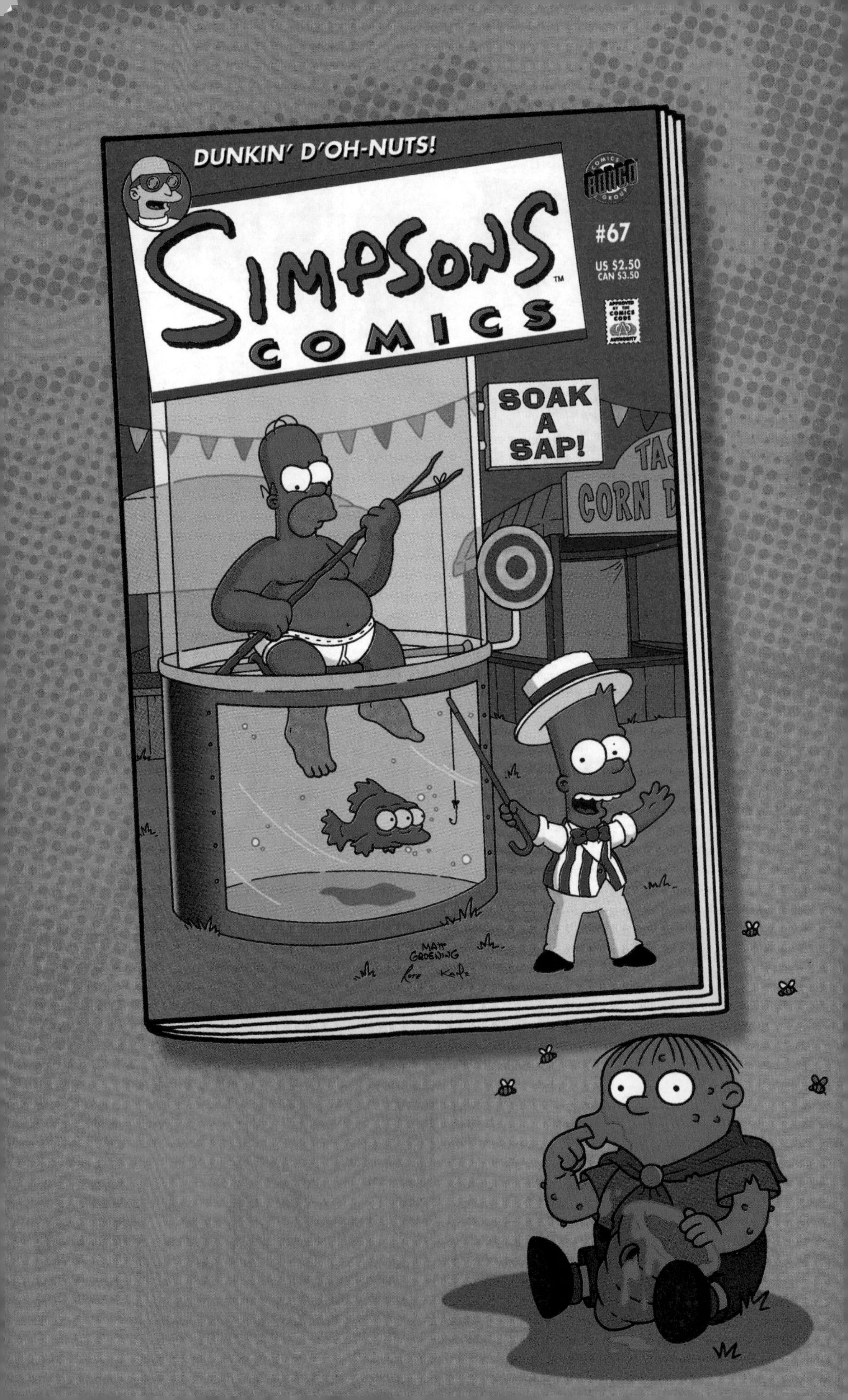

DUNKIN' D'OH-NUTS!

SIMPSONS COMICS

#67

US $2.50
CAN $3.50

SOAK A SAP!

CORN D

MATT GROENING

SPRINKLE! THIS BATTLE IS ENDANGERING INNOCENT CIVILIANS! SEE IF YOU CAN SUMMON A WEATHER FIELD TO SHIELD THEM FROM FLYING DEBRIS!

I WILL DO AS YOU SAY, OCTOCLOPS ...BUT I DO NOT UNDERSTAND WHY WE MUST PROTECT THOSE WHO ONLY HATE AND PERSECUTE US!
I DON'T HATE HER!
I DON'T WANT TO PERSECUTE HER AT ALL!

SPRINKLE! QUESTION OUR FATE NOT, FOR AS EVER, OUR BATTLE MUST DO SUCH THAT WE MAY STRUGGLE TOWARDS WHAT IS EVER AND SO SHALL ALWAYS IT MUST BE EVER THUS. SUCH IS THE PLIGHT OF THE Z-MEN!

WELL, THEM ARE SOME MIGHTY PURTY WORDS, PERFESSOR--BUT RIGHT NOW, I GOTS ME A CRITTER NAME O' BUCKTOOTH TO SKIN!
SNOKT!

WELL THEN, WHY DON'T YOU QUIT YAKKIN' AND BRING IT ON, SHORTY!

YOU GOT IT, PAL!
WEASELRINE, NO!!!
CHUNNNKKK!!
AARRGGHHH!!

GROWING PAINS!
DAD! YOU'RE WIPING YOUR BIG, DUMB FACE WITH MY Z-MEN COMIC!
Z-MEN MOVIE SPECIAL
GAIL SIMONE STORY
PHIL ORTIZ PENCILS
TIM BAVINGTON INKS
ART VILLANUEVA COLORS
KAREN BATES LETTERS
MATT GROENING MR. GREEN JEANS

THERE ARE STILL LUMPS IN MY BA-SGHETTI!
...AND THAT'S THE ULTRA-RARE CHROMIUM VARIANT COVER! LIZARD MAGAZINE SAYS THERE ARE LESS THAN TEN MILLION COPIES OF THAT BOOK IN PRINT!
BUT THE TRIPLE-THICK MANDO PAPER IS SO SUPER-ABSORBANT!
MOM, DON'T FORGET, YOU AND DAD PROMISED TO TAKE ME TO MY ENVIRO-BEARS MEETING TONIGHT.
LIZARD
I REMEMBER, SWEETIE. HOW IS YOUR LITTLE CLUB DOING, BY THE WAY?
NOT TOO GOOD, MOM. PEOPLE JUST DON'T SEEM TO TAKE ANY PRIDE IN SPRINGFIELD ANY MORE. IT'S LIKE, ONCE YOU START TALKING ABOUT THE ENVIRONMENT, PEOPLE JUST SEEM TO...
HOMER!
SPROING!
ZZZZZZZZZZZZZZZZ
...AND ANOTHER CELEBRITY I THINK MIGHT BE A TRANSVESTITE IS THAT TALK SHOW GUY WHO ALWAYS WEARS A DRESS! NOW, I DON'T HAVE ANY REAL FACTS TO BACK ME UP--IT'S JUST A GUT FEELING!
Z-MEN
POINK!
DAAAAAD! WE WERE TALKING ABOUT BEAUTIFYING OUR TOWN!
...AND YOU STILL OWE ME A COMIC, HOMER!
MY GARLIC TOAST NEEDS MORE WARM MILK IN IT!

NOW, BART, I HAVE IN MY POCKET FOUR SHINY QUARTERS. YOU CAN GO AND BUY SEVERAL NEW COMICS, AND MAYHAP A FESTIVE PENNYWHISTLE, AND STILL HAVE TUPPENCE REMAINING!

THAT COMIC COST $7.50, HOMER.
D'OH!!

LISA! BART! I THINK I HAVE A WAY TO SOLVE BOTH YOUR PROBLEMS, EVEN THOUGH I'VE ALREADY FORGOTTEN WHAT LISA'S PROBLEM IS! TO THE BASEMENT, BOY!
WHEN I WAS A BOY, COMICS WERE MADE OF FIBER-GLASS, AND YOU HAD TO WEAR SPECIAL GLOVES TO READ 'EM! "SCRATCHY DREADFULS," WE CALLED THEM.

SEE, BOY, YOUR OLD MAN'S A THINKER! NOT ONLY DID I SAVE THE VERY FIRST COMIC I EVER BOUGHT, BUT I EVEN STORED IT IN A PLASTIC BAG TO KEEP IT IN MINT CONDITION!

GUESS I SHOULDN'T HAVE USED A SANDWICH BAG. ENJOY, SON!
BUT, DAD...!
THE Z-MEN
NOW, DON'T GO ALL MILHOUSE ON ME, BOY. THE LOOK IN YOUR EYES IS THANKS ENOUGH.

RASSA FRASSA STINKIN' DUMB OL' PIECE O' JUNK FUNNYBOOK, ANYWAY!

WELL, THAT'S ONE FAMILY CRISIS AVERTED IN MY OWN COMICAL STYLE. AND NOW, IT'S FINALLY HOMER-TIME. WHERE'S THAT REMOTE?

HOMEY, YOU PROMISED THAT YOU'D DRIVE US TO LISA'S CLUB MEETING TO-NIGHT, REMEMBER?
OF COURSE I REMEMBER! AND I INTEND TO KEEP THAT PROMISE, EVEN IF IT MEANS SITTING HERE ON THE COUCH AND WATCHING TV ALL NIGHT!

I MEAN IT, HOMER. YOU TURN OFF THAT AWFUL GEORGE CARLIN AND GET IN THE CAR!
BUT MARGE...! THIS IS THE ONE WHERE HE'S ANGRY AT THE SYSTEM! IT'S THE ONE WITH ALL THE OUTRAGEOUS OBSERVATIONS!
...AND HERE ARE SEVEN WORDS YOU CAN'T SAY ON TV...TWENTY FIVE YEARS AGO!

IT'S NOT LISA'S FAULT YOU'RE TOO LAZY TO PUSH THE RECORD BUTTON ON THE VCR...
LAZY LIKE A FOX, MARGE! I JUST HAD THE GREATEST IDEA EVER BY A HUMAN!
GREATER THAN PENICILLIN?
PENICILLIN STINKS. LISA, GO GET ME SOME MORE EXTENSION CORDS.

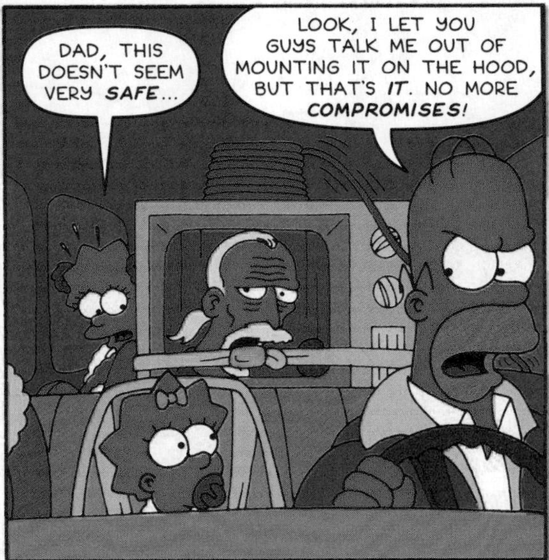
DAD, THIS DOESN'T SEEM VERY SAFE...
LOOK, I LET YOU GUYS TALK ME OUT OF MOUNTING IT ON THE HOOD, BUT THAT'S IT. NO MORE COMPROMISES!

I THINK THE EXTENSION CORD IS ABOUT TO RUN OUT!
THAT'S RIGHT, LISA. TV IS MAGICAL!
...AND ANOTHER THING I HATE IS KIDS WITH TERMINAL ILLNESSES. WHY IS IT ALWAYS "ME, ME, ME" WITH THEM?

SOON...
KID'S ENVIRONMENTAL MEETING
TUESDAY
POPSICLE STICK SCULPTURE SALE-A-BRATION!
NOT...ONE... WORD...

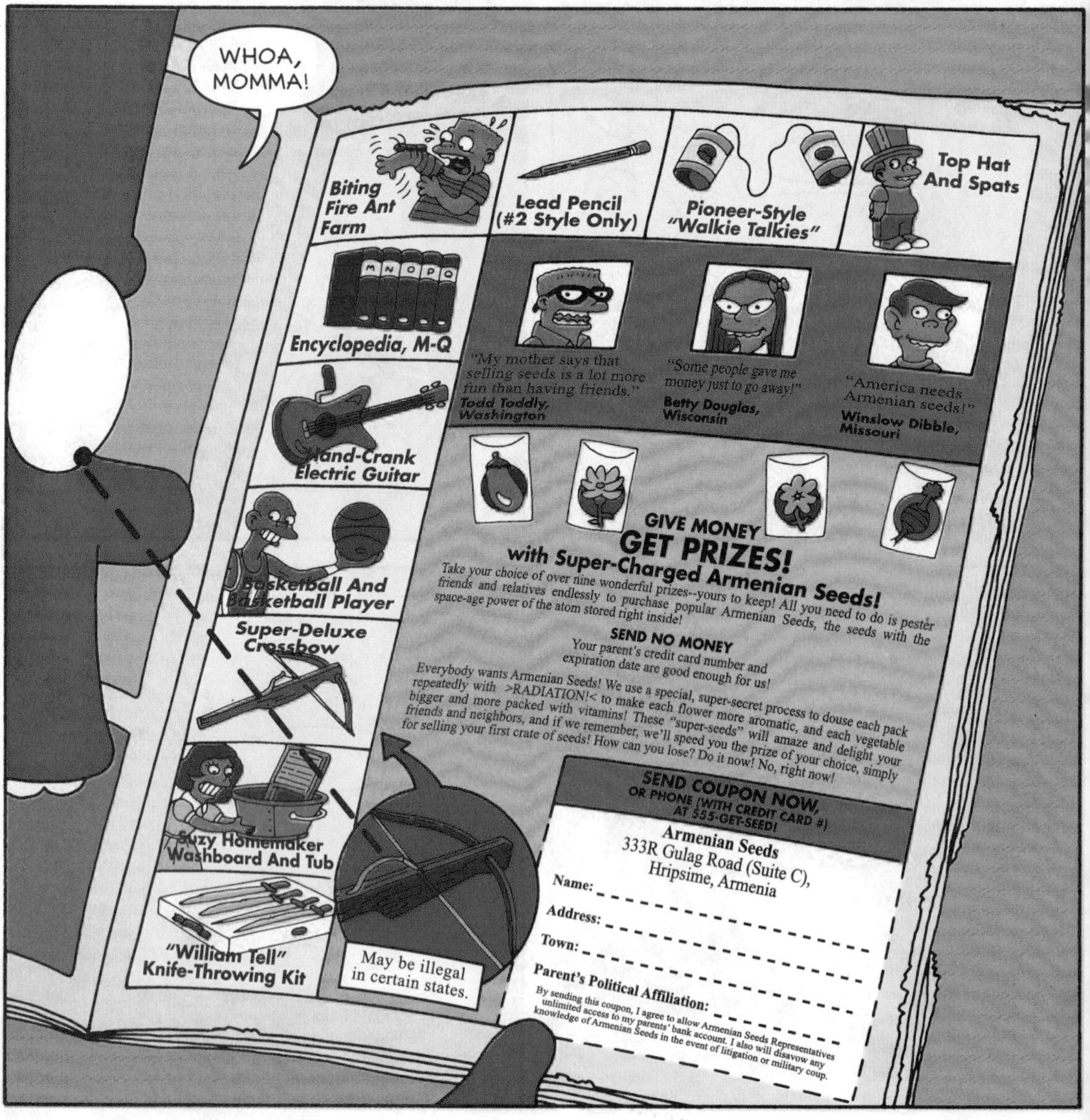

WHOA, MOMMA!

Biting Fire Ant Farm
Lead Pencil (#2 Style Only)
Pioneer-Style "Walkie Talkies"
Top Hat And Spats
Encyclopedia, M-Q
Hand-Crank Electric Guitar
Basketball And Basketball Player
Super-Deluxe Crossbow
Suzy Homemaker Washboard And Tub
"William Tell" Knife-Throwing Kit

"My mother says that selling seeds is a lot more fun than having friends."
Todd Toddly, Washington

"Some people gave me money just to go away!"
Betty Douglas, Wisconsin

"America needs Armenian seeds!"
Winslow Dibble, Missouri

GIVE MONEY
GET PRIZES!
with Super-Charged Armenian Seeds!

Take your choice of over nine wonderful prizes--yours to keep! All you need to do is pester friends and relatives endlessly to purchase popular Armenian Seeds, the seeds with the space-age power of the atom stored right inside!

SEND NO MONEY
Your parent's credit card number and expiration date are good enough for us!

Everybody wants Armenian Seeds! We use a special, super-secret process to douse each pack repeatedly with >RADIATION!< to make each flower more aromatic, and each vegetable bigger and more packed with vitamins! These "super-seeds" will amaze and delight your friends and neighbors, and if we remember, we'll speed you the prize of your choice, simply for selling your first crate of seeds! How can you lose? Do it now! No, right now!

SEND COUPON NOW,
OR PHONE (WITH CREDIT CARD #) AT 555-GET-SEED!

Armenian Seeds
333R Gulag Road (Suite C),
Hripsime, Armenia

Name: - - - - - - - - - -
Address: - - - - - - - - - -
Town: - - - - - - - - - -
Parent's Political Affiliation: - - - - - - -

By sending this coupon, I agree to allow Armenian Seeds Representatives unlimited access to my parents' bank account. I also will disavow any knowledge of Armenian Seeds in the event of litigation or military coup.

May be illegal in certain states.

LISTEN, MAN, I WANT THAT CROSSBOW, AND I DON'T CARE HOW MANY CRATES OF SEEDS I HAVE TO SELL TO GET IT! GOT IT?
HEY! THERE'S NO TV! IS THIS 1947?

YOU'RE REALLY ORDERING, YOU SAY? YOU WOULDN'T KID OL' GIL, NOW, WOULD YA, KID?
HOT DOG! AND MOTHER WANTED ME TO STAY HOME THIS WEEK!
ARMENIAN SEED CO.
ARMENIAN SEED CO.
ARMENIAN SEED CO.

HEY, BUTCH! THIS KID WANTS THE FULL PACKAGE! GIL'S SHIP FINALLY CAME IN! PUT OL' GIL UP ON THE BIG BOARD!
ARMENIAN SEED CO.
ARMENIAN SEED CO.

SALES
1999
2000
2001
1
YEAH, SURE, WHATEVER.

...AND I'M AFRAID WE'RE FALLING SHORT ON OUR GOAL TO END WORLD POLLUTION AND GLOBAL WARMING. ALSO, WE GAVE THE LAST $1.50 IN OUR TREASURY TO REVEREND LOVEJOY FOR THIS MEETING'S REFRESHMENTS.

HEY, IT'S NOT AS IF ORANGEADE GROWS ON TREES, LISA SIMPSON!

LET'S FACE IT, EVERY-ONE. IF WE DON'T THINK OF A WAY TO **RAISE** SOME FUNDS, WE'LL HAVE TO **SHUT DOWN** THE ENVIRO-BEARS FOR **GOOD!**
OOOH, I **HATE** GOATAL WARMING! IT MAKES LISA SAD!

WELL, WHAT IF, SAY, SOMEONE **ACCIDENTALLY** ROBBED A FEW GAS STATIONS, AND MAYBE THEY, **HYPO-THETICALLY,** "DONATED" THE PROCEEDS? **FIGURATIVELY SPEAKING,** I MEAN?
KEARNEY, THAT'S A LOVELY THOUGHT, BUT I DON'T THINK YOU SHOULD BREAK THE LAW TO SAVE OUR CLUB.

YOU FIGURED OUT THAT I MEANT **ME,** RIGHT?
RIGHT.
DANG!

KIDS, DON'T WORRY! I JUST THOUGHT OF THE GREATEST IDEA OF ALL TIME!
BETTER THAN PENICILLIN, MR. SIMPSON?
MOST PEOPLE **HATE** PENICILLIN, MILHOUSE. BUT **THIS** IDEA'LL RAISE A **TON** OF MONEY FOR YOUR CLUB!

NO, HOMER. NO **STREAK-A-THONS**. IT DIDN'T WORK FOR **MONDALE,** AND IT WON'T WORK NOW.
D'OH.

SORRY TO BREAK THIS UP, KIDS, BUT I'VE GOT A TRUNKFUL OF HARRY POTTER BOOKS TO **BURN** BEFORE ANY CHILDREN DISCOVER THE JOY OF READING...
OOOH! IT'S A DOUBLE-FEATURE, KIDS! THE REVEREND'S GONNA DO SOME OL' FASHIONED **BOOK-COOKIN'**!
HOORAY!
Harry Potter and the Sorcerer's Kidney Stone
I HAVE MY **SCHOOL BOOKS** IN THE CAR!

EVERYONE TRY TO THINK OF A MONEY-RAISING IDEA BEFORE NEXT WEEK'S MEETING, OKAY?
OH, SWEETIE, I'M SURE YOU'LL THINK OF SOMETHING.
YEAH, LIKE WHEN **JERRY LEWIS** BUSTED UP WITH **DEAN MARTIN**. HE WAS SO SAD, HE WENT RIGHT OUT AND INVENTED PENICILLIN!

ONE WEEK LATER...
SURELY THERE'S SOME **WACKY, MADCAP SCHEME** TO MAKE MONEY THAT WE HAVEN'T TRIED YET...
OH, WHO AM I KIDDING? I CAN'T EVEN GET PEOPLE TO CARE ABOUT SPRINGFIELD, OUR OWN HOMETOWN. I MIGHT AS WELL GIVE UP AND CALL THE OTHERS. ≈SIGH!≈

LISA, I'M GOING TO ASK YOU A FEW QUESTIONS, AND I NEED YOU TO BE HONEST WITH ME. FIRST, DID YOU KNOW THAT THE COST OF ILLEGAL CROSSBOWS HAS **SKYROCKETED** SINCE 1962?
BART...WHAT ARE YOU **TALKING** ABOUT?

NEVER MIND. DID YOU KNOW THAT DAD'S **CREDIT CARD** CHARGES **32%** INTEREST?
32%?!? ISN'T THAT **USURY**?
YOU'RE NOT HELPING, LIS...ONE MORE QUESTION...
BART, I DON'T LIKE THE SOUND OF THIS...

DO YOU KNOW ANY-ONE WHO NEEDS **10,000** PACKS OF SEEDS?
MROOWWR! HISSS!
RUTABEGAS
ARMENIAN SEEDS
DAISIES
POSIES

BART, YOU'VE GOT TO MAKE THE SEED COMPANY TAKE THEM ALL BACK!
I TRIED THAT! THEY JUST **LAUGHED** AT ME!
I'M SO DEAD. TRY TO GET THEM TO SCATTER MY ASHES IN APU'S SQUISHEE MACHINE.
VIOLETS

I'VE **GOT** IT! WE'LL GET THE ENVIRO-BEARS TOGETHER, AND WE'LL SELL THEM! IT'LL BEAUTIFY THE TOWN, AND WHAT MONEY IS LEFT AFTER PAYING OFF DAD'S CREDIT CARD WILL GO INTO THE CLUB FUND!
SCAT! SCAT!
VIOLETS
¡AIEE! ¡PERO NÉCTAR ES **BUENO**!

BART, GET ME MY **LUCKY CLIPBOARD**.
≈GASP!≈

SOON...
ER, UH, I'M SORRY, LITTLE GIRL, BUT I'M AFRAID I'M **TOO BUSY** POLLING MY CONSTITUENTS TO BUY YOUR, UH, COOKIES, OR WHATEVER...
TEE HEE!
MISS CONGENIALITY
SAMPLES
SLAM!

WE NOW TAKE YOU **LIVE** TO THE DOOR OF OFF-DUTY ANCHORMAN **KENT BROCKMAN**, WHERE HIS HEARTLESS REFUSAL TO PURCHASE SEEDS IS AS WE SPEAK CRUSHING THE **ENTREPRENEURIAL SPIRIT** OF THIS BRIGHT YOUNG MAN.
JEEZ, YOU COULD JUST SAY **NO**!
SAMPLES
SLAM!

SORRY, LI'L LISA, BUT I'M AFRAID I CAN'T BEAUTIFY MY GARDEN ANY MORE...I'M WALKING A **FINE LINE** BETWEEN GOOD CITIZENSHIP AND PRIDEFUL-NESS AS IT IS!
SAMPLES
SLAM!

DEFINE IRONY: A PRECOCIOUS TOT ATTEMPTING TO PROFIT OFF OF **ME**, INSTEAD OF T'OTHER WAY 'ROUND.
DOES THAT MEAN YOU'LL BUY SEEDS?
NO! FREAKIN' **KIDS!**
MAY THE FORCE BE
SLAM!

DOES YA HAVE ANY SKUNKY-CABBAGE, BLACK-EYED KUDZU, OR MAMA'S TEAT-MILKWEED?
UH, NO. WE HAVE BEGONIAS, THOUGH!
I CAIN'T FEED NO **BEGONIAS** TO MY FAMILY. THAT'S **DISGUSTIN'**!
SLAM!

WHOA, MAN! YOU HAVE **SEEDS**? WHERE WERE YOU FIFTEEN MINUTES AGO?
CLANG!

30-40-41-42...THAT'S IT, GANG. EIGHT DOLLARS AND FORTY-TWO CENTS IS ALL WE COLLECTED.
DON'T FORGET THAT **FIVE** OF THOSE DOLLARS CAME FROM AUNT PATTY IN RETURN FOR ME WEARING THIS **STUPID SAILOR SUIT** ALL DAY!
MY PRIDE AND TOES HURT.

WELL, I COLLECTED OVER **FORTY DOLLARS** IN THE SCHOOL CAFETERIA ALONE!
KEARNEY! THAT'S **WONDERFUL!** HOW DID YOU EVER...?
HEY, I CAN'T HELP IT IF SOME OF THE SMALLER AND MORE-EASILY-INTIMIDATED KIDS WANTED TO CONTRIBUTE THEIR LUNCH MONEY!

WELL, EVEN WITH ALL THOSE KIDS GOING HUNGRY, WE STILL AREN'T ANYWHERE NEAR OUR GOAL...
I'LL GET IT! IT MIGHT BE A LOST PIZZA DELIVERY BOY OR A DANGEROUSLY OVERLOADED GYRO TRUCK!
KNOCK! KNOCK!

KRACKA-BOOOM!!!
GASP!

AH, HELLO, CHILDREN. SELLING...**SEEDS,** I SEE. WELL, I'VE COME TO ASK YOU TO STOP IT. NO, I'VE COME TO DEMAND THAT YOU CEASE YOUR SEED-SELLING THIS INSTANT!

STOP SELLING SEEDS? BUT WHY, MR. BURNS?

LET ME MAKE THIS VERY CLEAR, CHILDREN. I AM **ALLERGIC** TO GROWING THINGS. DO YOU THINK I BUILT THE MOST TOXIC **NUCLEAR PLANT** IN THE COUNTRY ON ACCIDENT? **PISH TOSH!**
SO YOU WILL DESIST YOUR PETTY **SEED-SELLING TOM-FOOLERY** AT **ONCE!** FOR IF YOU DO NOT...

...I WILL TAKE **DRASTIC** MEASURES! YOU HAVE BEEN **WARNED**.

HMMM. DO YOU THINK I CAME ON A LITTLE STRONG WITH THOSE TYKES, SMITHERS?
NOT AT ALL, SIR! IT WAS A **MASTERFUL** PERFORMANCE!
EXCELLENT. I'D HATE TO THINK I FRIGHTENED THEM, BUT JUST IN CASE THEY DIDN'T LISTEN, BETTER WARM UP THE **DEATH RAY**.
RIGHTI-O, SIR!

SOON...
MARGE! THOSE SURLY ARMENIANS ARE REPOSSESSING OUR **HOUSE**!
IT'S JUST LIKE THAT PSYCHIC HOTLINE PREDICTED! HOMER, **STOP THEM!**
ARMENIAN SEEDS HOUSE REPO. CO.

ALL YOU HAVE TO DO IS PAY THIS **SEED BILL**, THEN YOU GET THE BITS OF YOUR HOUSE BACK.
FIFTEEN THOUSAND DOLLARS!???!?! BUT I DIDN'T EVEN **ORDER** ANY SEEDS!
FIRST STEP IS ADMITTING YOU HAVE A PROBLEM, MISTER.
IF YOU DON'T PAY BY **MIDNIGHT TOMORROW**, WE'LL BE BACK FOR THE **REST**.

DAD...IT'S MY FAULT. I WANTED A CROSSBOW. I DIDN'T KNOW **THIS** WAS GONNA HAPPEN! I'M SORRY, DAD...SNIFF!
HOMEY, WHAT ARE WE GOING TO **DO**? WE CAN'T LOSE OUR **HOUSE**!

IN MY DAY, WHEN THERE WAS A MONEY CRISIS, THE WHOLE **TOWN** WOULD GET TOGETHER AND HAVE AN OLD-FASHIONED **COUNTRY FAIR**!
THAT'S A GREAT IDEA, GRAMPA!
THAT'S THE DUMBEST THING I'VE EVER HEARD.

ON THE OTHER HAND, A TOWN FAIR IS THE BEST IDEA **EVER**!
BETTER THAN **PENICILLIN**?
WHAP!
FRED

HMM. A "**TOWN FAIR**," IS IT? WE'LL JUST SEE ABOUT **THAT**, MY MIDDLE CLASS FRIEND!
K-TEL'S Death Ray
LIP-READING FOR DUMMIEZ

THE NEXT DAY...
HEY, GUYS! CAN I COUNT ON YOU BOTH TO COME TO THE BIG TOWN FAIR TONIGHT?
SEED FAIR
MR. BURNS AIN'T GONNA BE TOO HAPPY WITH ANY OF HIS WORKERS GOIN' TO YOUR FAIR THERE, HOMER.
UMM...
WHAT? WHY DO YOU SAY THAT?

WELL, MAINLY ON ACCOUNTA THIS SIGNED DOCUMENT.
Notice of Intimidation
To all Plant Employees,
Regarding the so-called "Town Fair":
Anyone caught attending this repulsive tractor pull/hog-calling contest shall be soundly beaten and then dismissed, or otherwise harassed by thugs, and not those nice thugs shown in many delightful gangster comedies, either. That is all.
Sincerely,
C. Montgomery Burns

OH, SO YOU GUYS CAN'T DO ANYTHING WITHOUT MR. BURNS' APPROVAL NOW, IS THAT IT? WHAT IS HE, YOUR MOMMY OR SOMETHING?
HEY, THAT'S NOT FAIR! YOU WORK FOR MR. BURNS, TOO, YOU KNOW!
WHAT'S THE MATTER, LENNY? CAN'T TAKE THE HEAT WHEN MOMMY MCBURNS ISN'T AROUND?

YEP. YOUR MOMMY IS A WITHERED OLD MAN. IN YOUR FACE, CARL!
QUIT SAYING THAT, HOMER. IT'S DISTURBING!

HOMER SIMPSON SEEMS TO BE AGITATING YOUR WORKER BEES IN SECTOR 7-G, SIR.
REALLY? WELL, NOTHING OILS THE MACHINERY OF CAPITALISM LIKE SPIRITED DEBATE, YOU KNOW! BEST OF LUCK TO THAT RABBLE-ROUSING BEATNIK!
SHALL I HAVE HIM BEATEN, SIR?
OH, YES. THRICE, I'D SAY!

GOD BLESS THE FALL OF THE SOVIET SECRET POLICE. THESE BRIGHT YOUNG CHAPS COST ABOUT A THIRD OF WHAT MAFIA KNEE-BREAKERS NORMALLY CHARGE!
FFFSSSHHHH!
CLICK!

IS TARGET!
AIIIIEEE!
IS BONE-SMASH TIME! HIM GET! HIM GET!

HEY, YOU KNOW WHAT WOULD GO DOWN SMOOTH WITH THIS WATER?
NO, WHAT?

SOME SALTINES!
AW, YEAH, MAN. THAT'D BE SWEET.

AERIAL HIGH-FIVE FOR SALTINES!
YOU KNOW IT, BUDDY!

THOSE GUYS ARE GONNA KILL ME! IF ONLY MY BRAIN WEREN'T SO VERY...WHAT WAS I THINKING JUST NOW? SHUT UP, STUPID BRAIN! SHUT UP AND THINK!
TARGET IS GO THIS WAY, I AM THINK!

THUG MANEUVER #78B IS GO!
ANKLE-SNAPPING TACTIC ALPHA IS GO. REPEAT: IS GO WITH ANKLE-SNAPPING!
WARNING:

CARRAASSHH!!

?
COMRADE, IS DUMMY! IS NOT TARGET! OH, WE ARE FOOLED AGAIN. IS TIME TO ADMIT, WE ARE TERRIBLE AT THUGGING.
MMMPPHH!

WHEW! SAFE! BUT WHAT AM I GOING TO TELL LISA? WHAT AM I GOING TO TELL MARGE?
GATE #2
CAUTION: KEEP BURIED UNDERGROUND
RADIOACTI WASTE

IT'S A MIRACLE, HOMER! WE CALLED EVERYONE! THEY'RE ALL COMING TO OUR FAIR! EVERYONE'S COMING! AND THEY'RE ALL PITCHING IN TO HELP!
...HUH? BUT...BUT HOW'D YOU GET EVERY-ONE...?

TEARS, DAD! WE CALLED EVERYONE AND CRIED 'TIL THEY AGREED TO COME! WE CRIED FOR FOUR HOURS STRAIGHT! HAHAHA!
I GOT THE IDEA WHEN YOU DIDN'T PUNISH ME WHEN THOSE GUYS TOOK OUR STAIR-CASE! BOO-HOO, POOR LI'L ME, HAHAHAHAHA!

I'VE NEVER BEEN MORE PROUD OF YOU TWO! SNIFF!
NOW, GET SOME EYE DROPS, WE'RE GOING TO THE OLD-TIME TOWN FAIR!

THAT NIGHT...
gField Seed Fair
KNOCK-OVER THE MILK BOTTLES
CHOCOLATE-DIPPED BANANAS
SUMMER SQUASH SQUISHEE
THIS IS A SPECIAL EYE ON SPRINGFIELD FASHION REPORT, WHERE MY BLOODSUCKING DAUGHTER AND I WILL BE COVERING THE ENTIRE PRE-FAIR PAGEANTRY!
RIGHT YOU ARE, MOM! AND THAT MEANS WE'LL GET TO CALL SOME OF THE PEOPLE "PIGS" AND MAKE FUN OF THEIR HAIR AND SOME JUNK!

PONY RIDES
Kissing Booth
PIE AND GOSSIP
LEMONADE
OH! OH! WHAT FASHION NIGHTMARE IS THIS? I CAN'T LOOK! HELP! GET AWAY FROM ME, YOU BEAST! OH! OH!!!
HEY! MY MA'S BRIDE-Y DRESS DONE BE'D THE ONLIEST CLEAN THING IN THE SHACK TO WEAR TO SUCH A GALA AFFAIR!

SMITHERS! WHERE ARE THOSE GAY LIGHTS AND MERRY SOUNDS COMING FROM? THE TOWN SQUARE? SURELY THEY'RE NOT HAVING THEIR CURSED "FAIR" AGAINST MY WISHES?
AH...IT APPEARS SO, MR. BURNS!

HEY, MOE! HOW'S ***BUSINESS***?
UH, NOT TOO GOOD THERE, LISA. EVEN WITH THE ***FREE SEEDS*** I AIN'T SEEIN' NO ***ACTION***. I CAN'T FIGURE IT NO HOW!
Kissing Booth
Come and get him, ladies! Only 2 dollars!
KRAZY KAJUN SEED-FILLED FRITTERS

OH, GOOD LORD!
AAIIIEEE!
OH, RIGHT! THE ***FACE!*** I FORGOT MY UGLY ***FACE*** AN' ALL! NOW DON'T THAT BEAT EVERYTHING?

AND HEY, AIN'T YOU SUPPOSED TO BE OVER AT THE ***GAZEBO***? THEY BEEN LOOKIN' ***ALL OVER*** FOR YOU...SCOOT ALONG NOW OR THE FLAG WILL BE ***ROOINED!***
BUT I HAVEN'T SEEN THE FAIR YET!

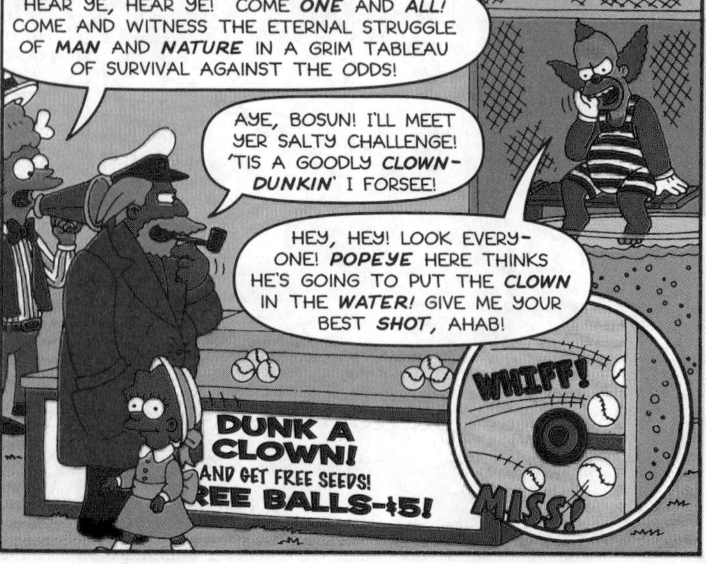
HEAR YE, HEAR YE! COME ***ONE*** AND ***ALL!*** COME AND WITNESS THE ETERNAL STRUGGLE OF ***MAN*** AND ***NATURE*** IN A GRIM TABLEAU OF SURVIVAL AGAINST THE ODDS!
AYE, BOSUN! I'LL MEET YER SALTY CHALLENGE! 'TIS A GOODLY ***CLOWN-DUNKIN'*** I FORSEE!
HEY, HEY! LOOK EVERYONE! ***POPEYE*** HERE THINKS HE'S GOING TO PUT THE ***CLOWN*** IN THE ***WATER!*** GIVE ME YOUR BEST ***SHOT***, AHAB!
DUNK A
CLOWN!
AND GET FREE SEEDS!
REE BALLS-$5!
WHIFF!
MISS!

HUH?!
KLAANGG!
AHA! YER KEELHAULED, MATEY!

SPLOOSH!
ARGH! MY AGENT SAID THIS WAS A NO-DUNK GIG!

JUST A MOMENT, ADMIRAL! I DETECT CHICANERY!

YOU ARE A SCOUNDREL THROUGH AND THROUGH, SIR! I ACCUSE YOU OF HIDING SEVERAL UNPAID-FOR BASEBALLS IN THAT POUCH OF SKIN!
HEY! SPUTTER! A LADDER MIGHT BE NICE, MAYBE! GLUB!

AYE, MY KANGAROO-LIKE POUCH IS MY SECRET SHAME, SAYS I. ARR.

EWWW!

♫ OH, SPRINGFIELD, OH SPRINGFIELD, ♫
WITH YOUR REMAINING GREENERY.
♪ OH, SPRINGFIELD, OH, SPRINGFIELD, ♪
WE LOVE YOUR ADEQUATE SCENERY.

WE LOVE YOUR AIR, THOUGH IT IS GRAY.
♪ WE TRY TO BREATHE IT, ANYWAY. ♪

♪ OH, SPRINGFIELD, OH SPRINGFIELD, ♪
♫ OUR DYING TOWN WE LOVE! ♫

YOU KNOW THAT THIS WILL ONLY KILL **PLANT LIFE**, RIGHT, SIR?

K-TEL'S Death Ray

KZZAAAPPP!

OF COURSE I KNOW IT, AND **THANK** YOU FOR REMINDING ME, SAMMY SPOILSPORT!

KZZZAAAPPP!
RUMBLE!
RUMBLE!
LOOK OUT!
GASP!

KA-BOOM!!
KA-BOOM!!
IS THIS THE END OF YE OLDE MILHOUSE?!

VO-YOIKS! THAT BEAM COMING FROM THE POWER PLANT IS MAKING THOSE IRRADIATED SEEDS HIGHLY UNSTABLE WITH THE BLOWING AND THE EXPLOSIVE-TYPE KABOOM-ING!
BAM!
WELL, THANK YOU, MR. EXPOSITION.

UH, I'M AFRAID THE DEATH RAY IS SOMEHOW MASSIVELY ACCELERATING THE SEEDS' GROWTH, MR. BURNS!
DRAT. IT'S LIKE NICARAGUA ALL OVER AGAIN.

LOOK OVER THERE!
THE SEEDS ARE GROWING LIKE CRAZY! IT'S BEAUTIFUL!
SPRINGFIELD COUNTY COURT HOUSE

POLICE
AW, WILL YOU LOOK AT THE LOVELY COLORS! I FEEL SO RENEWED!
I CAN TASTE IT WITH MY SNIFF-SNIFF!
POLIC

ARR, 'TIS A **TREE-BOAT** I HAVE NOW, I SEES. HANDSOME PETE AND I WILL BE BUNKIN' IN A PLACE OF **FLOWERY BEAUTY**, 'TIS TRUE.

CURSED ALLERGIES! QUICKLY, SMITHERS BRING ME MORE **POLLEN-FREE OXYGEN**!
YES, SIR!
OXYGEN

LOOK, MOM! WE RAISED **MORE** THAN ENOUGH MONEY TO PAY BART'S SEED BILL, AND WE BEAUTIFIED THE **WHOLE TOWN**!
OH, I'M SO **PROUD** OF YOU, SWEETIE!
YEAH, LIS...THANKS FOR SAVIN' MY BACON!

THE IMPORTANT THING IS WE GOT OUR **TOILET** BACK, AND NO ONE'S IN **JAIL**.

GOOD **LORD**! OUR TESTS INDICATE THAT THE RAY NOT ONLY MADE THE PLANTS GROW, IT MADE ALL THE ADULTS IN TOWN **INFERTILE**!
BEEP! BEEP!
HUH?

WHAT HE'S SAYING IS THAT NONE OF THE **GROWN-UPS** IN SPRINGFIELD CAN HAVE BABIES EVER AGAIN WITH THE **DIAPERS** AND THE **SMELLING** AND THE, **OH**, THOSE STRAINED PEAS!
BOOT! BOOT!

WELL, THEY DON'T HAVE TO BE SO HAPPY ABOUT IT!
THE END

THE ABOMINABLE DR. COLOSSUS
...AND IT IS MY PROFESSIONAL OPINION THAT DR. COLOSSUS POSES NO DANGER TO SOCIETY.
SPRINGFIELD MINIMUM SECURITY PENITENTIARY
TODAY'S LUNATIC ESCAPEE DANGER LEVEL IS: LOW

THAT IS A FILTHY LIE! I SHALL DESTROY SOCIETY! THIS DO I VOW!
THANK YOU, DR. STUBBS.

NOW, DR. COLOSSUS, WOULDN'T YOU AGREE THAT YOU ARE, IN FACT, COMPLETELY HARMLESS?
NO, I WOULD NOT!
HMMPH!

...AND IS IT NOT TRUE, DOCTOR, THAT IN ALL YOUR YEARS AS A MAD SCIENTIST, YOU HAVE REPEATEDLY FAILED IN YOUR ATTEMPTS TO CONQUER HUMANITY?
BAH! YOU HAVE INVOKED THE WRATH OF COLOSSUS!

IF YOU'RE LOOKING FOR THE CONTROLS TO YOUR COLOSSO-BOOTS, MAY I REMIND YOU THAT WE CONFISCATED BOTH THEM AND YOUR BELT OF EVIL WHEN YOU WERE REMANDED TO THIS FACILITY THREE YEARS AGO?
GGGGAAAAAH!
TAP!
TAP!
TAP!
TAP!

YOU FOOLS! IF I HAD MY BOOTS, I WOULD DESTROY YOU ALL!
I'M SORRY, DOCTOR, BUT WE NEED YOUR CELL FOR REAL CRIMINALS, LIKE TERRORISTS AND FORMER CHILD ACTORS.
YOUR PAROLE IS HEREBY GRANTED.

WE'LL ALL MISS YOU!
YEAH, BEST OF LUCK ON THE OUTSIDE, DOC. SINCERELY.
BYE, DOC!
WE ♥ KOLAWSUS!
BAH! YOU'LL PAY FOR YOUR INSOLENCE WITH COLOSSUS-INFLICTED DOOM!

I JUST WANT TO SAY, DOCTOR, THAT IT'S BEEN MY PLEASURE TO HAVE BEEN YOUR WARDEN HERE THESE LAST THREE YEARS. GOOD LUCK TO YOU!
BAH! COLOSSUS CARES NOT FOR YOUR DEMEANING WORDS! LEAVE AT ONCE, OR BE ANNIHILATED!
AWW, WE'LL MISS YOU, TOO, YA BIG LUG.
SNIFF!

DR. COLOSSUS NEEDS NO ONE! YOU SHALL ALL BE CRUSHED UNDER THE CRUSHING...UH... CRUSH POWER...
...OF MY MIGHTY...ER... CRUSHING BOOTS!
YOU WILL BEG AND PLEAD, BUT COLOSSUS WILL SHOW NO MERCY!

COLOSSUS NEEDS A RIDE INTO TOWN!

HA! DESPITE YOUR STERNLY-WORDED SIGNS, I WILL NEVER USE EXACT CHANGE! NEVER!
THE EVIL OF COLOSSUS KNOWS NO BOUNDS!
DEATH MOUNTAIN
YEAH, OKAY, WHATEVER.

NOW...IF I CAN ONLY REMEMBER WHERE THE LIGHT SWITCH OF TORMENT IS LOCATED.
I HOPE THOSE BATS DON'T ATTACK ME LIKE LAST TIME...
KLICK!

FLAP!
FLAP!
FLAP!
ACK! GAH! GURF!
FLAP!
FLAP!

SHORTLY...
MY REVENGE UPON THE WORLD THAT HAS SHUNNED ME BEGINS THIS VERY EVENING! BUT FIRST, I'LL NEED THE BOOTS FROM MY SPARE COSTUME!
ONLY THE GENIUS OF COLOSSUS COULD HAVE ENVISIONED SUCH SHOES OF TYRANNY!
SHISSSSSSH!
PAF!

AH, THERE YOU ARE. MY BOOTS, MY PRECIOUS BOOTS.
DID YOU MISS ME?

DON'T WORRY. DADDY'S HOME.
AH-HAHAHA HAHAHA!

GAAAAAH!
FLAP!
FLAP!
FLAP!
FLAP!
FLAP!

SO BEGINS THE DOCTOR'S REIGN OF TERROR! SOON, AT THE FIRST BANK OF SPRINGFIELD...
BEWARE THE WRATH OF COLOSSUS, SPRINGFIELD! THIS ENTIRE TOWN NOW BELONGS TO ME!
SO, YOU REFUSE TO HAND OVER THE MONEY? SO BE IT!
NOW BEHOLD THE AWESOME MIGHT OF MY COLOSSO-BOOTS!
CLICK!
KRUNCH!
BAH! THIS IS MERELY A SETBACK!
HO, HO! HA! HA! HA! HA! HOO! HA!

AT "LE SNOOTY JEWELERS DE SPRINGFIELD"...
AHA! BEING FRENCH, AZ I AM, I FIND YOUR SLAPSTICK POZITION MOST AMUZING! I DERIDE YOUR ZILLY, ZILLY FOOTWEAR! EH-HEH!
BAH!!

...THE KWIK-E-MART...
OH, PLEASE SIR! YOU ARE TICKLING MY BONE OF FUN WITH YOUR INCOMPETENT SUPER-VILLAINY, DON'T YOU KNOW!
BAH! I SAY AGAIN, BAH!
HA HA!

...CLETUS' HOUSE OF DISCOUNTED ROADKILL...
LOOKIE LOOKIE, BRANDINE! MR. FANCY-PANTS EVIL GENIUS DONE UP AND PUT HISSELF CLEAN THROUGH TO THE SECON' FLOOR OF OUR LI'L HOME BIZZYNESS!
BAH! BAH! BAH! BAH! BAH! BAH!!!
HOPE HE DON'T SPOOK THE MUSK OX NONE!

EXCUSE ME, SIR, BUT YOU ALREADY FAILED TO ROB THIS BANK YESTERDAY.
SIGH EVEN COLOSSUS FEELS THAT THIS IS A BIT PATHETIC.

CAN'T YOU, I DON'T KNOW...ARREST HIM OR SOMETHING? HE'S BECOMING A NUISANCE!
WHAT, ARREST OL' DOC COLOSSUS? AWW...

"...YOU DON'T REALLY WANT ME TO ARREST THE POOR GUY, DO YA? I MEAN, LET'S FACE IT..."
"...HE'S COMPLETELY HARMLESS."
SNIFF!

THANKS FOR THE RIDE, EDDIE.
HEY, CHIN UP, DOC! I'M SURE YOU'LL BE BACK TA COMMITIN' MAJOR CRIMES WIT' DEM BOOTS O' YOURS ANY DAY NOW! YOU TAKE HER EASY, ALL RIGHT?
BAH.
THAT'S THE SPIRIT!

YOU HAVE ONE MESSAGE.
HELLO, DR. COLOSSUS? THIS IS GENERAL KLAW FROM THE SECRET SOCIETY OF EVIL GENIUSES. I'M AFRAID WE'VE VOTED TO REVOKE YOUR MEMBERSHIP. YOU'RE JUST TOO EMBARRASSING. CALL ME, WE'LL PLAY BRIDGE SOMETIME.
SIGH.

IT'S TRUE. IT'S ALL TRUE. COLOSSUS IS A FAILURE AS A CRIMINAL MASTERMIND!
ALL I WANT IS TO CAUSE PEOPLE TO FLEE IN TERROR...IS THAT TOO MUCH TO ASK?

FLAP!
FLAP!
FLAP!
FLAP!
AACCK! SPUTTER! GAH! FILTHY CREATURES!

GAIL SIMONE STORY · **JOHN COSTANZA** PENCILS · **PHYLLIS NOVIN** INKS · **RICK REESE** COLORS · **KAREN BATES** LETTERS · COLOSSO-BOOTS SUPPLIED BY **MATT GROENING**

NOW WITH 15% MORE MILHOUSE!
SIMPSONS COMICS
#68
US $2.50
CAN $3.50
NOT ONLY DID YOU FAIL ALL OUR TESTS OF SKILL, FATTER-EATER LAD, BUT YOUR "SPASTIC COLON" IS NOT A BONAFIDE SUPER-POWER!
PERMISSION TO JOIN OUR CRIME-FIGHTING CLUB... DENIED!
CAPTAIN COMIX
THE KWIKSTER
YES
NO
YES
NO
YES
NO

IAN BOOTHBY STORY · PHIL ORTIZ PENCILS · PHYLLIS NOVIN INKS · ART VILLANUEVA COLORS · KAREN BATES LETTERS · MATT GROENING HERO AT LARGE

I SAW YOU SHOPLIFT THAT WATCH!

YEAH, WELL I SAW YOU SHOPLIFT THREE COFFEE MUGS, A ROLODEX, AND FIVE HAIR SCRUNCHIES.

PLEASE! YOU CAN'T TURN OL' GIL IN! I NEED THIS SECURITY JOB! I HAVE COCKFIGHTING GAMBLING DEBTS!
WELL, I'LL LET YOU OFF WITH A WARNING THIS TIME!

GOSH, THANKS MISTER! YOU WON'T REGRET IT!
HI-DIDDILY-HO, GIL! ANY LUCK NABBING THOSE PESKY SHOPLIFTERS TODAY?

NONE, MR. FLANDERS, SIR.
WELL, GOSH-DIDDILY-DARN IT! THOSE FIFTH COMMANDMENT BREAKERS ARE BLEEDING ME DRIER THAN A COMMUNION WAFER!
MUGS

MEANWHILE...
I DO NOT UNDERSTAND IT. THE SQUISHEE SUPPLY IS EMPTY AGAIN, YET WE HAVE NOT SOLD ONE DELICIOUS CUP ALL DAY!
MÄLK
MÄLK
E
F

D-DUDE! THE RUBBER PANTS WERE A G-G-GREAT IDEA!
Y-YEAH. AND I HARDLY THINK ABOUT G-G-GIRLS AT ALL ANYMORE!

ELSEWHERE...
GOT A SHIPMENT OF RADIOACTIVE MAN'S HERE!
UH... *I'LL* SIGN FOR THOSE!
THE HAPPY LITTLE ELVES

HEH, HEH!

WAIT! WAIT! CURSE MY NEED TO VISIT THE "*DANGER ROOM*" EVERY TEN MINUTES!
I BLAME *YOU*, EXTRA LARGE MOUNTAIN DEW!

YEAH, I HEAR YA! SHOPLIFTING IS A *TERRIBLE THING*, BUT I'M AFRAID I'M *HELPLESS* TO DO ANYTHING!

HEY, LOU! THE CHIEF'S *FALLEN ON HIS BACK* AGAIN!
HE'S SO *CUTE* WHEN HE DOES THAT!
HEY, GUYS! LITTLE HELP?

LATER...
A *BAG* OF PORK RINDS, APU, MY GOOD MAN!
HERE YOU ARE, MR. HOMER, SIR!
THAT WILL BE *$400*

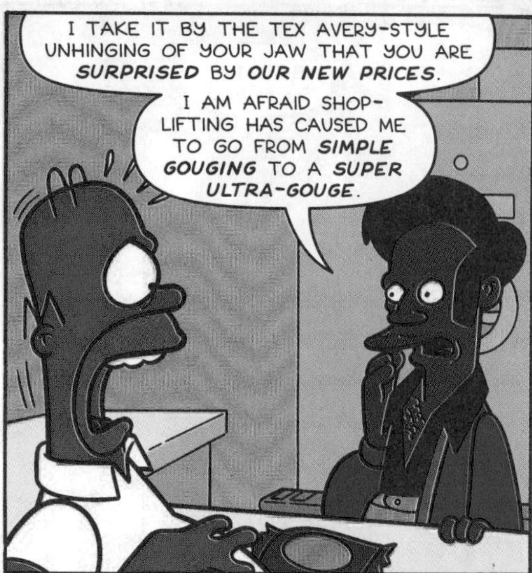
I TAKE IT BY THE TEX AVERY-STYLE UNHINGING OF YOUR JAW THAT YOU ARE *SURPRISED* BY *OUR NEW PRICES*.
I AM AFRAID SHOP-LIFTING HAS CAUSED ME TO GO FROM *SIMPLE GOUGING* TO A *SUPER ULTRA-GOUGE*.

SO ANGRY!
GOTTA GO TO MOE'S AND CALM DOWN!

HEY, HOMER!

WHY SO GLUM, BARNEY?
AW, I GOT A **MONKEY ON MY BACK!**

I THOUGHT YOU **STOPPED** DRINKING.
I DID.

THE MONKEY'S **CIGAR** IS BURNING THE BACK OF MY NECK!
OH, HEY! SORRY ABOUT THAT, HE'S HAD ONE TOO MANY **BANANA DAIQUIRIS!**

HERE YOU GO, HOMER!
BUT IT'S SO SMALL!
THAT'LL BE **$100!**

YEAH, YEAH, I'VE SEEN YOU UNHINGE YER JAW BEFORE.
LISTEN, I GET MY PEANUTS AND PICKLED EGGS FROM THE **KWIK E-MART**. NOW THAT **THEY'VE** JACKED UP PRICES, I GOTTA DO THE SAME.

PEOPLE OF SPRINGFIELD, ARE YOU GOING TO STAND FOR SHOPLIFTERS TAKING AWAY OUR RIGHT TO EAT AND DRINK OURSELVES TO DEATH?
I SAY WE MARCH ON THE MAYOR'S OFFICE!
HEY, HE'S GOT A POINT!
YEAH, YOU TELL US, HOMER!

SOON...
MR. MAYOR, YOUR WEEKLY ANGRY MOB IS HERE.
IS IT TUESDAY ALREADY?
HEALING, NOT STEALING
THIS SPACE FOR YOUR AD CALL 555-8245
DOWN WITH SHOPLIFTING

SEND THEM...ER, AH...IN.

MR. MAYOR, WE NEED YOU TO CRACK DOWN ON SHOPLIFTING!
I...AH... WISH I COULD HELP.

BUT ACCORDING TO OUR...AH, LATEST POLL, MOST PEOPLE IN SPRINGFIELD CONSIDER SHOPLIFTING TO BE AN...ER, VICTIM-LESS CRIME.
WE HAD TO SHUT DOWN OUR VICTIMLESS CRIME UNIT MONTHS AGO.
VERY FEW PEOPLE WERE PRESSING CHARGES.

WE HAVE SOMETHING TO SAY!
WHO...?

IF YOU, THE CITY, WILL FUND US, THEN WE SHOPKEEPERS WILL DEFEND OURSELVES BY TAKING THE LAW INTO OUR OWN HANDS.
THE POLICE WON'T HAVE TO LIFT ONE FAT FINGER!

WILL THIS BE...ER...COOL CHARLES BRONSON-STYLE VIGILANTE JUSTICE?
YES!
MAN, I REALLY HAVE BEEN LETTING MY FINGERS GO.

FUNDING GRANTED!
HOORAY!

LATER, IN NED'S FLANDERS' BASEMENT...
WE ARE NOW A LEAGUE OF EXTRA-ORDINARY GENTLEMEN FIGHTING FOR TRUTH, JUSTICE, AND THE CAPITALIST WAY! WE NEED A CATCHY NAME TO CONVEY FEAR AND RESPECT!
I PROPOSE "THE MERCHANTS OF VENGEANCE"!
THAT'S A TAD TOO VIOLENT FOR MY TASTES. AND VENGEANCE IS ALREADY SOMEONE ELSE'S DEPARTMENT.

HOW ABOUT JUSTICE FOR JESUS?
UM...NO!

ANTI-PUNK PATROL!
THE HOLY HELPERS!
CAPTAIN COMIC BOOK AND HIS ALL-STAR SHOPKEEPERS!

I COULDN'T HELP OVERHEARING YOUR BRAINSTORMING SESSION.
HERE'S A NAME OUR FOCUS GROUPS LOVED!
WHAT ARE YOU DOING IN MY RUMPUS ROOM?
SYNERGIZING!

"THE BETTER BUSINESS BATTALION!" I LIKE IT!
AS DO I!
DITTO FOR ME!

I GOTTA HAND IT TO YOU, STRANGER, I--
HEY, WHERE DID SHE GO?

PERHAPS SHE WAS NEVER HERE AT ALL.
A MANIFESTATION OF OUR COLLECTIVE UNCONSCIOUS?
OR AN ANGEL.

SORRY, DID I MISS SOMETHING? I HAD TO USE THE RESTROOM.
CURSES! A GHOST CHICK WOULD HAVE REALLY ADDED TO OUR ORIGIN STORY!

SOON, THE CLERK CRUSADERS PUT THEIR PLAN INTO ACTION, WITH CUTTING EDGE GADGETRY!
MAN, APU'S NEVER AROUND. THIS IS *TOO EASY,* MAN.

CLICK!
CHUTN

WHAT'S UP WITH THE NOZZLE?

YAAAA!
FWOOOOOOOSH!

I MUST SAY, YOUNG DOLPH, FOR ONE ABOUT TO BE ARRESTED FOR SHOP-LIFTING YOU CERTAINLY KNOW HOW TO *KEEP YOUR COOL.*
"KEEP YOUR COOL." HEH, HEH. I MUST SUBMIT THAT TO THE *KWIK-E-MART NEWSLETTER'S* "HUMOR AT WORK" SECTION.

MEANWHILE...
WHOA, A LEFT-HANDED COMB! THAT'D BE GREAT FOR HAIR-RELATED GROOMING!
TIME FOR A *FOUR-FINGER DISCOUNT*.

ALERT! ALERT! INITIATING LIVE VIDEO FEED!

JIMBO!
WE'RE SO *DISAPPOINTED!*
MOM! GRANDMA! NO! THIS CAN'T BE HAPPENING!

WELL, THERE'S ONE *FINGER WAGGING* THAT LAD WON'T SOON FORGET.
SOB!
SALE

AND...
I THINK YOU WILL FIND THE COMICS YOU ATTEMPTED TO STEAL WERE *PRE-TREATED* TO DELIVER TEN TIMES MORE *PAPER CUTS* THAN THE LEADING BRAND!
AAAH!
GAH!

NOW, ARE YOU GOING TO TURN YOURSELVES OVER TO THE *PROPER AUTHORITIES,* OR DO I HAVE TO BRING OUT...

...*THE LEMON JUICE*?
AAAH! NO MAN! PUT THAT THING AWAY!
WE'LL GO TO THE COPS RIGHT NOW! SEE, WATCH US GO!

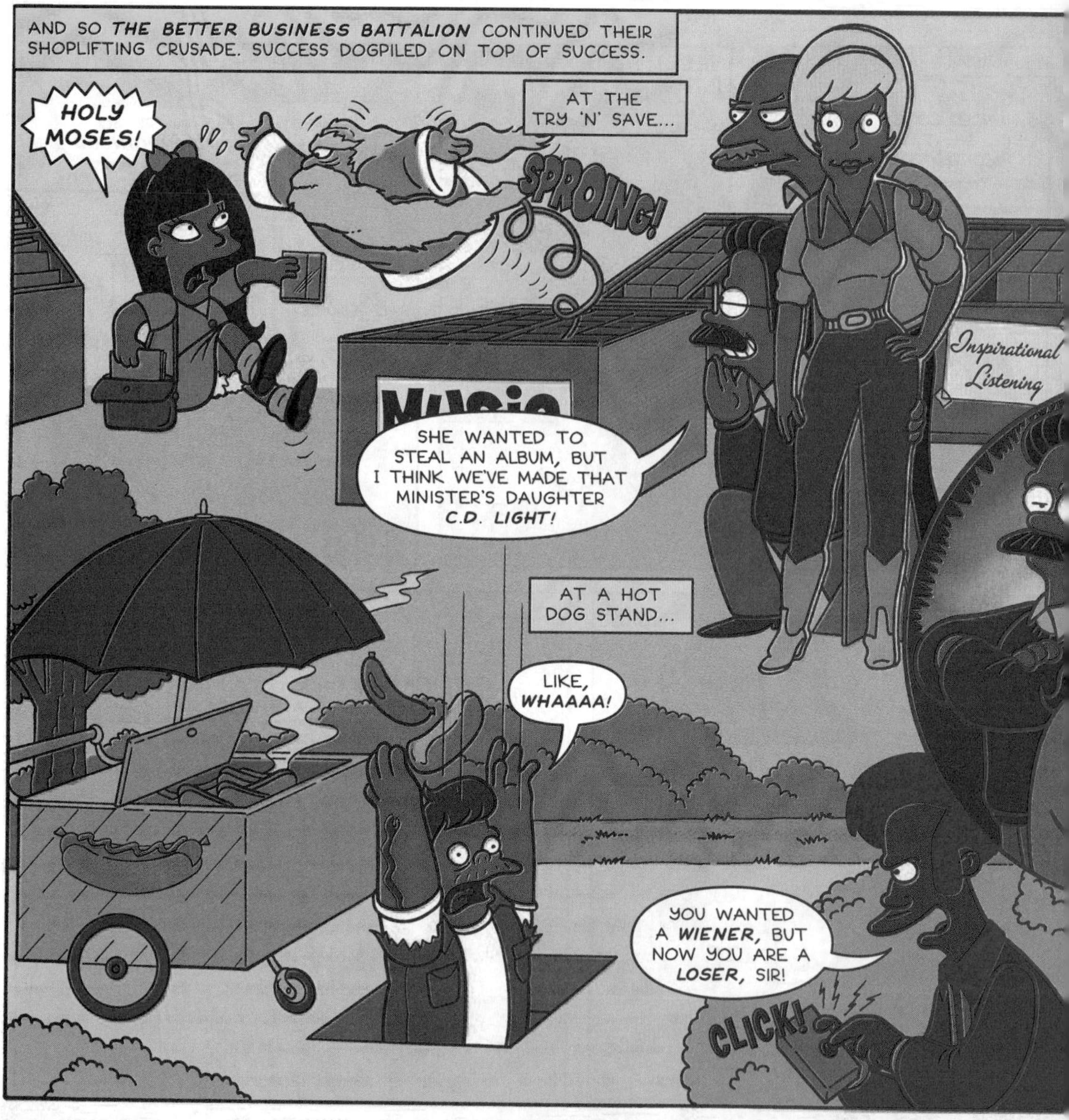

AND SO *THE BETTER BUSINESS BATTALION* CONTINUED THEIR SHOPLIFTING CRUSADE. SUCCESS DOGPILED ON TOP OF SUCCESS.

HOLY MOSES!

AT THE TRY 'N' SAVE...

SPROING!

Inspirational Listening

SHE WANTED TO STEAL AN ALBUM, BUT I THINK WE'VE MADE THAT MINISTER'S DAUGHTER ***C.D. LIGHT!***

AT A HOT DOG STAND...

LIKE, **WHAAAA!**

YOU WANTED A ***WIENER,*** BUT NOW YOU ARE A ***LOSER,*** SIR!

CLICK!

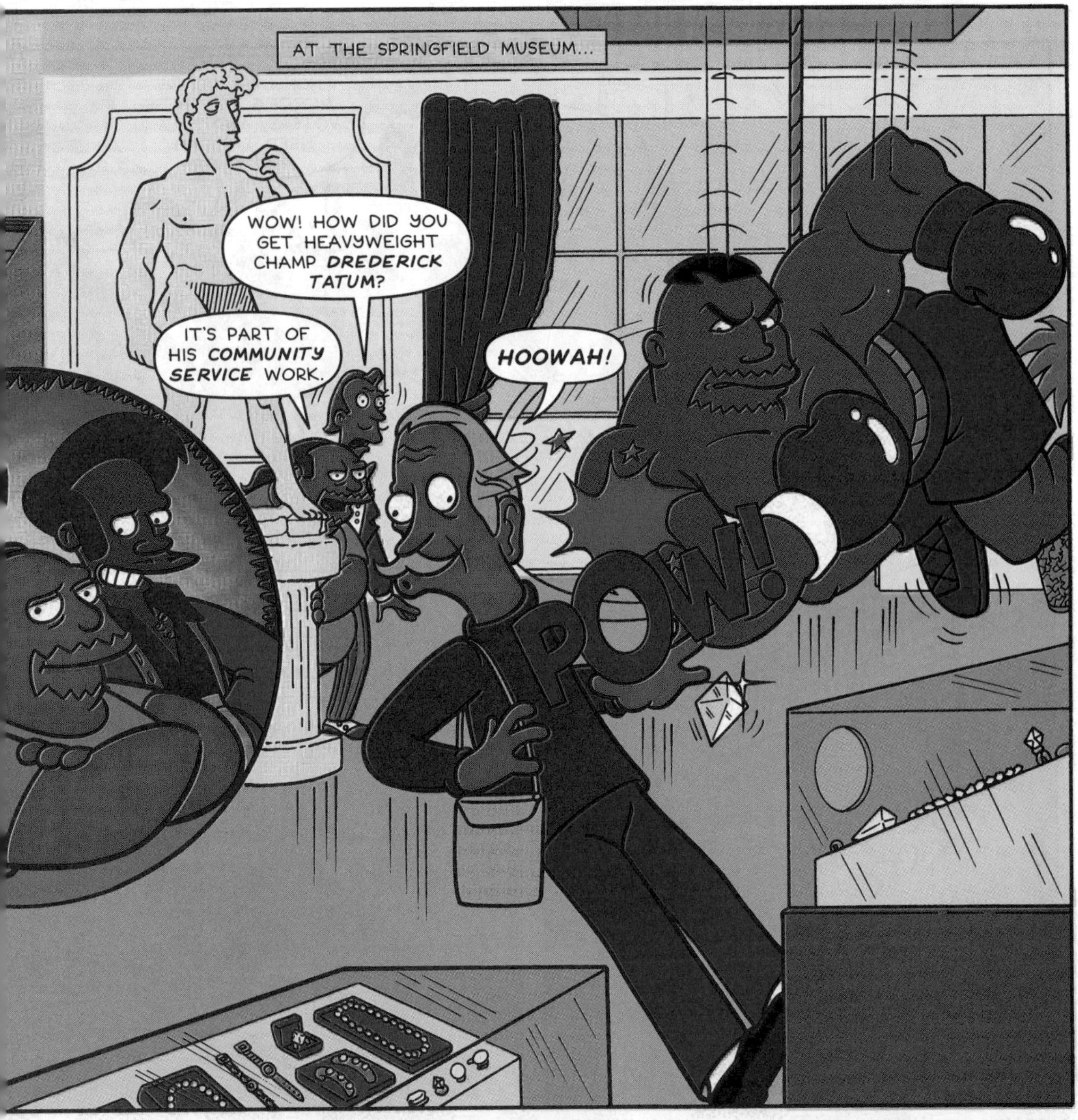

AT THE SPRINGFIELD MUSEUM...

WOW! HOW DID YOU GET HEAVYWEIGHT CHAMP **DREDERICK TATUM?**

IT'S PART OF HIS **COMMUNITY SERVICE** WORK.

HOOWAH!

POW!

TWO WEEKS LATER...
A PARADE IN OUR HONOR? DON'T YOU THINK THIS IS A LITTLE MUCH, MR. MAYOR?
NONSENSE. YOU'RE HEROES TO THESE VOTERS, AND I...ER... NEED THE...AH, PHOTO OP!
IT...ER...AH, APPEARS YOU HAVE FANS!

THE NEXT DAY...
WELCOME TO THE TRYOUTS FOR NEW B.B.B. MEMBERS. WE WILL CONDUCT THE TRIALS USING THE LEGION OF SUPER-HEROES' METHOD.
PRESENT WHAT YOU HAVE TO OFFER TO THE TEAM AND WE SHALL JUDGE YOU.
CAN WE TALK FOR ONE DIDDILY OF A SECOND?
LATER.
APU
NED
YES
NO
YES
NO
YES
NO

AAR! I'D BE HONORED TO JOIN YER CREW!
DIDN'T YOU APPEAR ON A BOX OF POISONED FISH STICKS?
AH, THERE'S A FUNNY STORY BEHIND THAT SENSELESS TRAGEDY!
NEXT!

WE DON'T WEAR COSTUMES.
OH THIS LITTLE NUMBER IS FOR A PARTY LATER. IT'S THE ACTUAL SUIT WORN BY THE PUZZLER IN THE 1960'S RADIOACTIVE MAN TV SERIES. ISN'T IT THE LIVING END?
SILVER AGE
SORRY, YOU'RE TOO CAMP!
NEXT!

I...
NEXT!

NOT ONE MET OUR HIGH STANDARDS OF EXCELLENCE. OH, WELL, WHAT SHALL WE DO TONIGHT FELLOW CRIME FIGHTERS?
YOU TELL HIM, MR. NED. WE AGREED YOU WOULD TELL HIM.
RARE COMICS
TELL ME WHAT? HEROES DON'T KEEP SECRETS FROM EACH OTHER.
APU
NED

IT'S JUST THAT THERE'S NO MORE CRIME. DAVID DIDN'T STICK AROUND AFTER HE BEAT GOLIATH.
WE'RE NOT NEEDED ANY-MORE.

BUT...THE GROUP. WHAT ABOUT US?
WE HAVE DONE OUR JOB, SIR.
YOU SHOULD BE AS PROUD AS IS ALLOWED WITH-OUT IT BECOMING A SIN.

WE WISH TO RETIRE WITH CLASS AND DIGNITY, LIKE THE BANGLES, NOT OVER-STAY OUR WELCOME IN SHAME, LIKE THE GO-GOS.

IF THERE'S EVER TROUBLE, YOU KNOW WHERE TO FIND US.
GOODBYE. I SHALL STILL HONOR YOUR B.B.B. 10% SQUISHEE DISCOUNT UNTIL THE END OF THE MONTH.

BUT WHAT WILL I DO?

JUST GET BACK TO YOUR LIFE.

ISOTOPES

YES, JUST GET BACK TO MY LIFE.

THE NEXT WEEK...
OPEN
396
THIS YOUNG SHOPLIFTER MUST HAVE THOUGHT IT WAS SAFE TO RETURN TO A LIFE OF CRIME!

BUT THAT WAS BEFORE HE MET *THE B.B.B. BUMPER STICKER BLASTER!*
THAT'S SOME NICE APPREHENDING, MR. G!
CLOSED
I GROK SPOCK!
My other car is a Klingon Warbird!

I JUST GOT THE GOOD WORD! YOU'VE CAUGHT *FIVE* SHOP-LIFTERS IN JUST ONE WEEK.
I SUPPOSE WE WERE *TOO HASTY* IN BREAKING UP OUR GROUP.
THEN WE'RE BACK?

AS LONG AS SHOP-LIFTERS THREATEN OUR COMMUNITY, WE'LL BE THERE.
HUZZAH!

UH, HUH! WELL, IF *I* WERE YOU, I'D JUST TELL AUSTRALIA TO EAT MY SHORTS.
BART! LISA! THE *SCHOOL BUS* IS HERE!
GOTTA GO, HOMER!

MAN, THE BUS SURE IS *EMPTY* TODAY.
EVERYONE'S BEEN *ARRESTED* FOR SHOP-LIFTING. IT DOESN'T MAKE SENSE.
DOLPH, NELSON, KEARNEY I CAN SEE...

...BUT MILHOUSE? MARTIN? SHERRI AND TERRI?
WELL, TERRI I CAN SEE. SHE'S THE EVIL TWIN, RIGHT?

SOMETHING'S GOING ON, BART.
AW, YOU'RE JUST BEING PARANOID.

I HOPE SO.

LATER...
AH, NOTHING LIKE AN AFTER SCHOOL SQUISHEE TO WASH AWAY THE BITTER TASTE OF LEARNING.

NEW KRUSTY KARAMEL KRUNCH? THIS I GOTTA TRY.
BUY!
KRUSTY KARAMEL KRUNCH

ALERT!
ALERT!
WHAT THE...?

GAAAH!
BANG!
CRUNCH!

OH, LITTLE BART SIMPSON. WHAT SHAME HAVE YOU BROUGHT ON YOUR FAMILY THIS DAY?
I DIDN'T DO IT...

YES, YES, WE ALL KNOW YOUR CATCHPHRASE, SHOPLIFTER.
SHOPLIFTER? I DIDN'T STEAL ANYTHING!

LET US ALLOW THE SECURITY TAPE TO END THIS DEBATE.

OH, NO!
OH, YES! NOW PLEASE WAIT HERE WHILE I CALL THE POLICE.

LOOK! IT'S VISHNU!

GASP! HE HAS ESCAPED! I AM SO ANNOYED I AM TEMPTED TO NOT EVEN SAY...
...THANK YOU. COME AGAIN!

LIS', YOU GOTTA HELP ME!
BART? WHAT IS IT?

I'VE BEEN ACCUSED OF A CRIME I DIDN'T COMMIT!
OH, GREAT, I'LL BET SOME-ONE'LL BLAME IT ON THE ONE-ARMED MAN AGAIN!

MINUTES LATER...
AND THAT'S THE WHOLE STORY. I'M INNOCENT I TELLS YA!
I BELIEVE YOU, BART. BUT WE NEED PROOF.

DING! DONG!
IT'S THEM!
KEEP QUIET! NO ONE KNOWS YOU'RE HERE.

HELLO THERE, MARGE. SORRY TO BE A BITHER-BOTHER, BUT IS BART HOME?
NO, HE ISN'T.

NOW IT'S NOT THAT WE DON'T TRUST YOU, BUT...
...TURN IT ON FELLAS!

AYE CARUMBA!
MY WORD!
AHA! THE BATTALION'S SUPER X-RAY-O-SCOPE FLUSHES OUT THE EVILDOER!

RUN!!!
LEAP!

TO THE B.B.B.MOBILE!
WE'RE ALREADY IN IT!
THEN ATOMIC BATTERY TO POWER AND TURBINES TO SPEED, APU!

JUST DRIVE THE RV.
WHY DID YOU NOT SAY SO IN THE FIRST PLACE?
VROOOM! VROOOM!

WHERE DID THEY GO?
AUSTRALIA DECLARES WAR ON NEW ZEALAND

GASP!
HUFF! PUFF!

LISA, I DON'T WANT TO GET YOU IN TROUBLE, TOO. I'M GONNA TURN MYSELF IN.
OKAY!

OKAY? YOU'D LET ME TURN MYSELF IN? DON'T YOU KNOW A BLUFF WHEN YOU HEAR ONE? NOW HELP ME!
OKAY, OKAY! LET'S GO BACK TO THE SCENE OF THE CRIME AND LOOK FOR CLUES.

LATER...
THE KWIK-E-MART SHOULD BE CLOSED AS LONG AS APU'S LOOKING FOR YOU.
PUT IT IN!
HERE'S THE SECURITY TAPE OF ME.
NACHO CHEEZ™
Cheese Substitute

HMMMM...
YOU SEE SOMETHING?

MAYBE, I...
FREEZE!

IN THE WORDS OF THE BORG, "RESISTANCE IS FUTILE, PUNKS!"

WE'LL GO QUIETLY, BUT PLEASE JUST WATCH THE SECURITY TAPE ONE MORE TIME!

WELL, OKAY, BUT ONLY IF THERE ARE SNACKS.

SOON...
WATCH CAREFULLY.

HE'S AS GUILTY AS GREEDO!
LOOK CLOSER. THIS HAPPENED AFTER SCHOOL AROUND SUNSET. THERE'S THE SHADOW OF THE POTATO CHIP STAND.

WHERE'S BART'S SHADOW?
HE'S A GHOST!
GASP!

NOT A GHOST, BUT A COMPUTER-GENERATED IMAGE USED TO FRAME MY BROTHER!

THERE'S NO PROOF I DID IT!
LOOK IN THE LOWER LEFT CORNER OF THE SCREEN.

"BART SIMPSON FRAMING© B.B.B. VISIT OUR WEBSITE AT WWW.FRAMINGBART.ORG"
OKAY, OKAY I CONFESS!

YOU TOLD ME TO LIVE MY LIFE, BUT THIS GROUP WAS MY LIFE.
FOR THE FIRST TIME EVER I FELT ACCEPTED, EVEN, DARE I SAY IT... LOVED.

I WANTED TO BE A MARTIAN MANHUNTER, BUT I ENDED UP A HAL JORDAN.
I ONLY HOPE YOU CAN FORGIVE ME.

AW, HECK! I'D FORGIVE YOU EVEN IF THE BIBLE DIDN'T FORCE ME TO.
YOUR KARMA IS CLEAR WITH ME AS WELL.
WELL I'M STILL MAD!

WHAT IF I GAVE YOU YOUR CHOICE OF ANY RADIOACTIVE MAN BACK ISSUE IN MY STORE?
SIGH YES.
EVEN HIS *ULTRA-RARE TEAM UP WITH CHAIRMAN MAO?*

COMMIE CRISIS!
JERKY
DEAL!
JERKY

CAN I OFFER ANYONE A RIDE HOME IN THE B.B.B.--I MEAN THE FLANDERS MOBILE?

WELL, IT WAS A FUN RIDE, NO ONE GOT HURT, AND EVERYTHING WORKED OUT FINE!

WAS THAT MR. FLANDERS' VAN?

NO TALKING IN *THE CHAIN GANG!*
YES, SIR!
THE END

MONEY TO BURNS!
SIMPSONS COMICS
#69
US $2.50
CAN $3.50

IN BURN$ WE TRU$T
SMITHERS, LOOK! MY AUTOBIOGRAPHY IS THE NUMBER ONE BEST-SELLER!
CONGRATULATIONS, SIR.
Sale $20.00
WILL THERE EVER BE A RAINBOW?
#1
C.M. BURNS
A SOUL-SHAKING SAGA OF BIBLICAL PROPORTIONS BROUGHT TO YOU BY:
IAN BOOTHBY STORY
HORACIO SANDOVAL PENCILS
STEVE STEERE, JR. INKS
ART VILLANUEVA COLORS
KAREN BATES LETTERS
BILL MORRISON EDITOR
MATT GROENING ARCHBISHOP OF BONGO

THAT NON-FICTION DISCOUNT BIN IS A TOUGH MARKET TO CRACK!
REMAINDER
"ALL BOOKS 5¢"

I'LL TAKE ANOTHER 100 COPIES FOR MY KRUSTYBURGER RESTAURANT.
OKAY, BUT UH...WHY?
ART

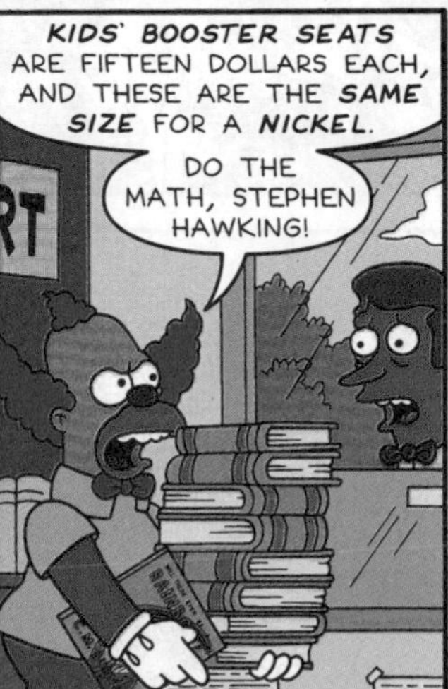
KIDS' BOOSTER SEATS ARE FIFTEEN DOLLARS EACH, AND THESE ARE THE SAME SIZE FOR A NICKEL.
DO THE MATH, STEPHEN HAWKING!

A SWEET VICTORY INDEED. AND YET...I CRAVE MORE. SMITHERS, WHAT'S THE BEST-SELLING BOOK OF ALL TIME? WE'LL CRUSH THAT AUTHOR LIKE A BUG!

THAT WOULD BE THE BIBLE, SIR.
GAAHHH!

I TAKE IT WE WON'T BE DOING ANY CRUSHING TODAY?
NO, THIS CALLS FOR A SIMPLE CHANGE OF PLAN. IF YOU CAN'T BEAT THEM...

"...JOIN THEM!"
SPRINGFIELD CHURCH
NOW WITH 25% MORE DOGMA

SNAP! SNAP!
I FEEL THE LORD! I FEEL THE LORD! DOWN IN MY HEART!

THIS VISITING CATHOLIC CHOIR IS VERY GOOD!
I DETECT THE INFLUENCE OF **MONK, BASIE,** AND **DEPECHE MODE**. MOST IMPRESSIVE!

SAY, ISN'T THAT THE **VEGAS LOUNGE SINGER** THAT WE SAW ON THE **NEWS**?
WHO?
YOU KNOW, THE ONE IN THE **WITNESS PROTECTION PROGRAM** WHO WAS GOING TO GIVE INSIDE INFORMATION ON **THE MOB**.

DA KID'S RIGHT!
GET HER!

BANG!
BANG!
SIGH! CAN'T WE GO **ONE MONTH** WITHOUT A **SERMON** ENDING IN **GUNPLAY**?

AND IF THAT WASN'T BAD ENOUGH, THE COLLECTION PLATE IS BARER THAN J. LO'S MIDRIFF.
NED, YOU ALONE TITHE MORE THAN THIS!

SORRY, REVEREND. I INVESTED ALL MY SAVINGS IN EVANGELICAL DOT COM STOCK.
WE NEED MONEY PEOPLE! THIS PLACE NEEDS A LOT OF WORK!

REMEMBER WHEN BART SIMPSON SMASHED OUR STAINED GLASS WINDOWS OF THE APOSTLES AND WE CUT CORNERS BY HIRING LENNY TO REPLACE THEM? HE DID A FINE JOB BUT...

...THE CAST OF "THE DREW CAREY SHOW" WAS NOT WHAT I HAD IN MIND!

MAYBE IT'S MY FAULT THAT WE'VE LET THINGS GO AROUND HERE.
THREE HELLFIRE SERMONS ON TITHING PER MONTH MAY BE TOO MANY. PERHAPS A LITTLE MORE TIME SPENT ON THE FUNDAMENTALS WILL PRY OPEN YOUR POCKETBOOKS.

TELL YOU WHAT. I'M GOING TO OPEN THIS SERVICE UP TO ANY QUESTIONS YOU HAVE ABOUT THE MYSTERIES OF OUR FAITH.

I'VE GOT ONE! IF YOU DRINK HOLY WATER AND TAKE A WHIZ ON A VAMPIRE, WILL YOU KILL HIM?

WHAT NAME DOES GOD SCREAM WHEN HE STUBS ***HIS*** TOE?

WHY ARE THE PEARLY GATES ALWAYS ***GOLD*** IN CARTOONS WHEN PEARLS ARE OBVIOUSLY WHITE?

WHAT DOES THE H. IN "JESUS H. CHRIST" STAND FOR?

WHY AM I SEEN ***SO FREQUENTLY*** IN THIS CHURCH WHEN I AM CLEARLY ***NOT*** A CHRISTIAN?

HOW MUCH MONEY WILL IT TAKE TO ***BUY*** YOUR CHURCH?
GASP!

MR. BURNS!
I'M AFRAID THIS CHURCH IS ***NOT FOR SALE!***

OH, THAT'S A PITY. REMOVE THE MONEY, SMITHERS.
BACK IN THE LIMOUSINE, SIR?
NO, THAT'S TOO MUCH TROUBLE. JUST ***BURN IT*** IN THE PARKING LOT.

WAIT! WHILE THE CHURCH ISN'T **FOR SALE**...
...THERE'S NOTHING IN THE BIBLE AGAINST...

...**SPONSORSHIP!**
EXCELLENT!

GOOD LORD, ⁑CHOKE!⁑

SOON...
EXODUS
I DON'T THINK I LIKE THE IDEA OF MR. BURNS SPONSORING THE CHURCH.
OH, MARGE! EVERYTHING HAS A SPONSOR. THE **BIG OIL COMPANIES** SPONSOR THE **GOVERNMENT** AND THAT'S ⁑COUGH⁑ WORKED OUT ⁑HACK⁑ FINE!

HELLO, SIR. ARE YOU HAPPY WITH YOUR RELIGIOUS SERVICE?
NOT REALLY.
WOULD YOU CARE TO SWITCH TO **WICCA** FREE FOR A MONTH?
WICCA, EH?

WE'RE HAPPY WITH OUR RELIGION, THANK YOU!
REMEMBER WHEN YOU BECAME A **MONK** FOR TWO MONTHS AFTER TALKING TO THAT **BUDDHIST**? I'M NOT GOING THROUGH **THAT** AGAIN.

THE NEXT WEEK...
AS YOU CAN SEE, THE STAINED GLASS WINDOWS HAVE BEEN **CHANGED**. MR. BURNS TELLS ME THIS IS JUST **TEMPORARY** AND THE APOSTLES ARE **ON ORDER**.
1.
2.
3.
4.
5.
HEY, LOOK! THERE ARE ONLY **FIVE** COMMAND-MENTS NOW!
WHEW! THAT'S **WAY EASIER** TO REMEMBER.

REVEREND, MAY I SAY A FEW WORDS?
WELL, I...
TAKE FIVE, PADRE!

AS YOU CAN SEE, I'VE MADE A **FEW CHANGES**, AND I THINK YOU'LL **ENJOY** THEM.

HEY, EACH PEW HAS A **MAKE YOUR OWN TACO BAR!**
NOW THAT'S **GOOD RELIGION!**

ONE SMALL THING. IT'S NOW A **SIN** TO BELONG TO THE **FOLLOWING ORGANIZATIONS**...
...THE ENVIRONMENTAL PROTECTION AGENCY, GREEN-PEACE, AND LISA SIMPSON'S TREE HUGGING SOCIETY.

WHAT? WHY I...
QUIET, **SINNER!** LEST YE DAMN US ALL!

YOU SEE, CHURCH IS LIKE A BOOK CLUB WHERE EVERY WEEK THEY TALK ABOUT THE SAME BOOK.
WHAT WOULD OPRAH THINK ABOUT THAT?

NOW, THE BIBLE IS A FINE...
AHHHH! IT BURNS!
HOLY BIBLE

AS I WAS SAYING, THE BIBLE IS A FINE BOOK, BUT SO ARE OTHERS LIKE...
...WELL...MY AUTOBIOGRAPHY FOR ONE.
HOLY BIBLE

WE'LL TALK ABOUT THIS FOR A MONTH OR TWO...
...THEN MOVE ON TO THE AYN RAND COLLECTION AND JOSEPH STALIN'S "HOW TO WIN FRIENDS AND CRUSH ENEMIES".
RAINBOW?
RAINBOW?

THIS IS HORRIBLE!
I KNOW. I'D LIKE TO PROTEST, BUT THE IDEA OF A MANDATORY BOOK CLUB IS JUST TOO APPEALING.

WELL I'VE HAD JUST ABOUT ALL I CAN STAND. ROD! TODD! WE'RE LEAVING!

FINE! GO!
BUT ONCE YOU LEAVE, YOU CAN NEVER COME BACK!

!

I'M WARNING YOU...

SOON...
SO YOU NEED A NEW RELIGION, HUH?
I FEEL SO EMPTY INSIDE.
THEN, BROTHER, YOU CAME TO THE RIGHT PLACE. IT'S GREAT BEING JEWISH!

THE FOOD'S GOOD, AND THERE'S MORE HOLIDAYS THAN YOU CAN SHAKE A STICK AT.
COME WITH ME!

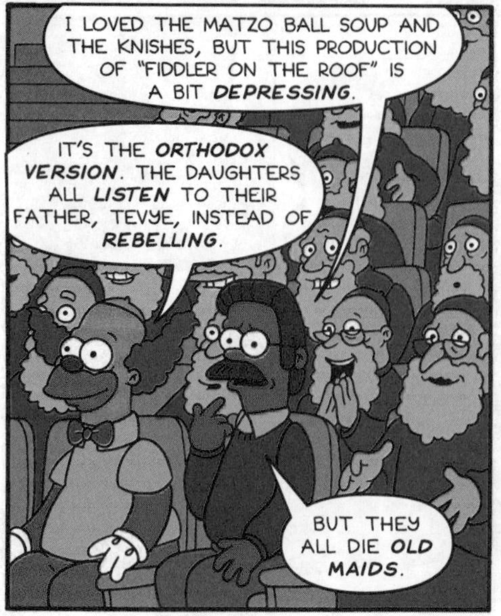
I LOVED THE MATZO BALL SOUP AND THE KNISHES, BUT THIS PRODUCTION OF "FIDDLER ON THE ROOF" IS A BIT DEPRESSING.
IT'S THE ORTHODOX VERSION. THE DAUGHTERS ALL LISTEN TO THEIR FATHER, TEVYE, INSTEAD OF REBELLING.
BUT THEY ALL DIE OLD MAIDS.

C'MON, LET'S GET OUT TO THE SNACK TABLE BEFORE ALL THE KUGEL'S GONE!
WELL DONE.
EXCELLENT!
CLAP!
CLAP!
CLAP!
CLAP!
CLAP!
CLAP!
I PARTICULARLY ENJOYED THE LACK OF DANCING.
CLAP!
CLAP!

I DON'T KNOW. I JUST DON'T THINK THE SHOE FITS ME.
YOUR LOSS.
BUT IF YOU CHANGE YOUR MIND, HERE'S A **COUPON** FOR A BUY-ONE-GET-ONE -FREE **BRIS**.

LATER...
THE LIFE OF A HINDU IS A **PEACEFUL** AND **FULFILLING** ONE!

WHAT? I CAN'T **HEAR** YOU OVER YOUR CRYING CHILDREN, THE CASH REGISTER, AND GUNFIRE!
WAAAAAH!
CH-CHING!
BANG!
BANG!
WAAAAA!
DUDE! I'M LIKE TOTALLY IN A **RUSH**.

I SAID THE LIFE OF A HINDU IS A **PEACEFUL** AND **FULFILLING** ONE!

SIGH!
NO LOITERING!
POW!
Duff
OPEN
Duff

EVEN LATER...
YOU REALLY SHOULD CONSIDER SNAKE HANDLING AS YOUR NEW RELIGION!
HSSSSSSSSSS

AAAAAH!

HEY, NED, BE A PAL AND CALL 911, WOULD YA?
MAN, THE ONLY DAY I DON'T BRING MY KNIFE TO WORK!
HSSSSSSSSSSSSSSSSSSSSSSS

LATER STILL...
I CAN OFFER YOU A RELIGION OF BLISS AND CONTENTMENT.
WELCOME TO KRUSTY BURGER

HEY, AM I PAYING YOU TO CLEAN THE GREASE TRAPS OR RECRUIT FOR YOUR CULT?
TO CLEAN THE TRAPS ...SIR!
WELCOME TO KRUSTY BURGER

SIGH.

OOOF!
AAAH! SORRY!
CRASH!
EASY THERE! WHAT'S THE SUN-DAY RUSH?

WE'RE LATE FOR CHURCH, AND THE MINISTER IS AWFUL STRICT!

STRICT YOU SAY?
IS THIS OLD-TIME RELIGION?

REALLY OLD, YEAH!

MIND IF I TAG ALONG?
AS LONG AS YOU DON'T MIND LONG SERMONS AND HARD PEWS.

THANK YOU, LORD!

MEANWHILE...
WILL I EVER GET TO TALK?
I DON'T KNOW. MR. BURNS IS REALLY ENJOYING THIS. HE EVEN BUYS HIS CLOTHES AT "THE HOUSE OF SHARPTON" NOW.
BROTHERS AND SISTERS. I HAVE A PARABLE FOR YOU!
LOOK AT THE VIDEO MONITOR IF YOU WILL.

THE MAN
WHO PLANTED
ATOMS

"ONCE UPON A TIME THERE WAS A MAN WHO PLANTED ATOMS."
"HE WOULD THROW THEM HITHER AND YON!"

"THE ATOMS THAT FELL ON THE ROAD..."
"...WELL, NOTHING HAPPENED."

"THE ONES THAT FELL ON RICH SOIL..."
"...THE SAME. NOTHING! ZIP! NADA!"

"BUT THE ATOMS THAT FELL IN A WELL-MAINTAINED NUCLEAR FACILITY SUPPLIED CLEAN, EFFICIENT ENERGY FOR EVERYONE!"

I'M CONFUSED.
YOU'RE SAYING OUR SOULS ARE LIKE ATOMS?

NO! NO! NO! NUCLEAR ENERGY IS THE SOUL OF THIS TOWN!
IT WAS A SUBTLE ALLEGORY. IF YOU NEED ME TO BE AS HAM-FISTED AS C.S. LEWIS, I WILL BE!

LATER...
MR. BURNS, I'M AFRAID THIS JUST ISN'T WORKING OUT.
I AGREE.
YOU DO? WELL, THAT'S A RELIEF. YOU SEE...

YOU'RE FIRED!
WHAT?!!

BUT YOU CAN'T FIRE ME!
I'VE PAID TO RENOVATE THE ENTIRE CHURCH IN THE LAST TWO WEEKS. THERE'S NOT AN ORIGINAL BRICK OR BOARD OF WOOD LEFT.
I OWN THIS BUILDING. PLUS I'M BRINGING THE CROWDS IN!

YOU ARE THE WEAKEST LINK. GOODBYE.

I DON'T GET THAT AT ALL.
IT'S A LINE FROM A POPULAR TELEVISION PROGRAM.
I DON'T WATCH TV.

NOT EVEN PBS?
WELL, YES...PBS.
THEN YOU WATCH TV. I HATE WHEN PEOPLE SAY THAT!
OH, JUST GET OUT!

MEANWHILE...
WELL BOYS, HOW ARE YOU ENJOYING THE SERVICE?
I DON'T KNOW DADDY. SOMETHING SEEMS WRONG.
I MISS OUR OLD CHURCH.

I DO TOO, TODD, BUT THIS IS THE **NEXT BEST THING**.

WHY DOES HE HAVE A **GOAT'S HEAD** ON HIS CHEST?
GOATS ARE GOD'S CREATURES TOO, SON.
HE SURE TALKS ABOUT **THE DEVIL** A LOT.
YOU CAN'T WARN FOLKS TOO MUCH ABOUT HIM! WE MUST ALWAYS **BE ON GUARD**.

LATER...
HEY, LISA, WANT TO GET SOME **ICE CREAM**? MY TREAT.
BART, WHERE DID YOU GET THE MONEY?

REVEREND LOVEJOY'S **THREE CARD MONTE GAME**.

REVEREND LOVEJOY! WHAT ARE YOU DOING?
LOSING MY SHIRT.
I'M BROKE, AND I HEARD THAT THIS WAS SUPPOSED TO BE A **SURE-FIRE MONEYMAKER**.

ARE YOU **CHEATING**?
OF COURSE NOT. THAT WOULD BE **WRONG**!

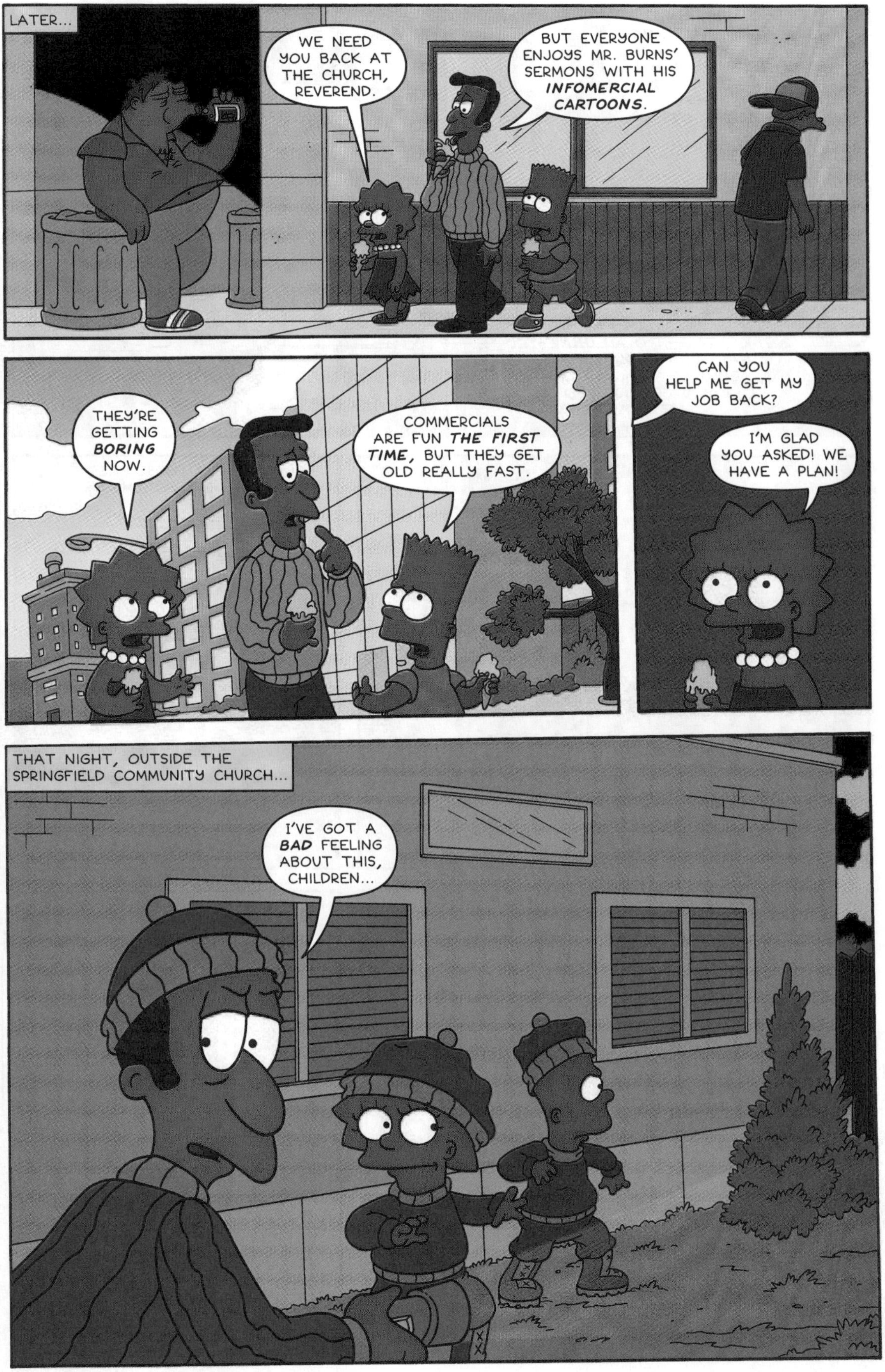

THAT NIGHT, OUTSIDE THE SPRINGFIELD COMMUNITY CHURCH...

I'VE GOT A **BAD** FEELING ABOUT THIS, CHILDREN...

BREAKING AND ENTERING JUST FEELS WRONG ...ESPECIALLY WHEN IT'S GOD'S HOUSE.
FELONIES ARE LIKE GETTING INTO AN UNHEATED SWIMMING POOL. DON'T THINK ABOUT IT AND JUMP RIGHT IN. YOU GET USED TO IT AFTER AWHILE.

LOOK AT THIS FILE! GASP!
IT'S MR. BURNS' MASTER PLAN.

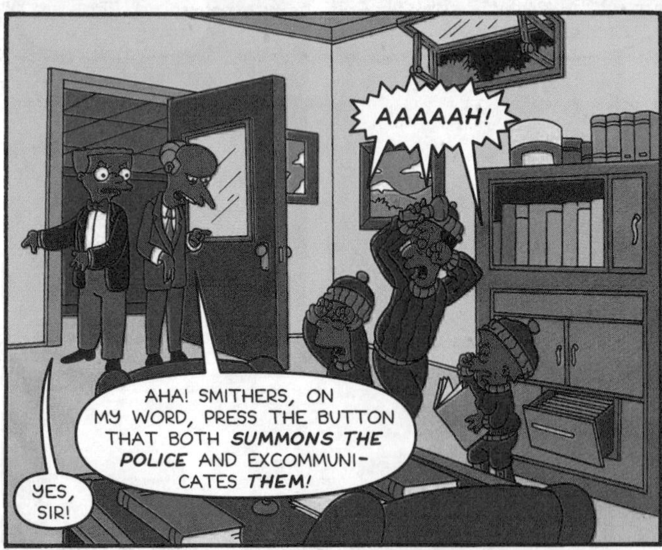
AAAAAH!
AHA! SMITHERS, ON MY WORD, PRESS THE BUTTON THAT BOTH SUMMONS THE POLICE AND EXCOMMUNICATES THEM!
YES, SIR!

ACCORDING TO THOSE FILES, YOU WERE USING MY CHURCH TO BECOME POPE?
IT STARTED WITH BOOSTING MY BOOK'S SALES, BUT THEN I GOT AN IDEA.

"LITTLE BY LITTLE I'D WORK MY WAY UP THE LADDER. ONE CHURCH AT A TIME UNTIL ONE DAY I WAS POPE."
"THEN I'D HAVE ACCESS TO ALL THE VATICAN GOLD AND JEWELS! AND IT'D ALL BE TAX-FREE!"

BUT THIS ISN'T A CATHOLIC CHURCH.

IT'S THE SAME BIBLE.
YES.
THE SAME SAVIOR?
YES.
BUT NO POPE?
NO.

SMITHERS WE'RE LEAVING. THIS RELIGION BUSINESS IS MORE CONFUSING THAN THE INTERNET.
YAY!

BUT FIRST, BEFORE I GIVE THE CHURCH BACK TO YOU, I'D LIKE YOU TO INDULGE ME.

CERTAINLY, WHAT CAN I DO?
AS I SAID. INDULGE ME. IN EXCHANGE FOR THE CHURCH BACK YOU'LL GIVE ME AN INDULGENCE.
YOU MEAN BUY YOUR WAY INTO HEAVEN? BUT THE CHURCH HASN'T DONE THAT IN YEARS.

IT'S STILL WITHIN YOUR JURISDICTION. I'VE MADE A FEW ERRORS IN MY TIME AND I NEED A GUARANTEE I'LL GET INTO HEAVEN WHEN I DIE.
JUST WRITE IT DOWN AND THE CHURCH IS YOURS.

EXCELLENT!
I'LL LEAVE A COPY FOR YOUR FILES AND BID YOU GOOD NIGHT!

I CAN'T BELIEVE YOU WROTE THAT!
READ THE CARBON COPY.

"I HEREBY GUARANTEE MR. BURNS' ADMITTANCE INTO DOG HEAVEN WHEN HE DIES."

DON'T MESS WITH A MINISTER!
HA! HA! HA! HA! HA! HA!
SMACK!

THE NEXT DAY...
SO YOU SAY ALL WE HAVE TO DO IS SIGN THIS CONTRACT IN BLOOD, AND WE'LL BE LIFELONG MEMBERS IN YOUR CHURCH?
AND BEYOND.
WELL, THAT'S SWE-DIDDILY-ELL!

DADDY, I...
NOT NOW, TODD. DADDY'S GOT TO SIGN THIS!
BUT DADDY!

LATER, TODD. LATER!

THIS IS A DEVIL CHURCH!

OH MY SWEET LORD! IS THIS REALLY A CHURCH OF SATAN?
OF COURSE, IT IS! IT'S **WRITTEN** ON ALL OUR **STATIONERY**.

RUN BOYS, RUN!

WELL, WE **SCARED** ANOTHER ONE OFF. IS IT **ME**?
DON'T BEAT YOURSELF UP, ROY.
WHO WANTS TO MAKE **TOLL HOUSE COOKIES**?

AW! YOU GUYS ARE **THE BEST**!

LATER...
WELCOME BACK TO THE FLOCK, NED.
THANKS, REVEREND. IT FEELS LIKE **HOME**! ARE THE TACO BARS STILL HERE?

NO, BUT NOW IF EVERY-ONE PAYS ATTENTION, I SPRING FOR **PIZZA** AFTERWARDS.
WHAT ARE **YOU** DOING HERE?
I HEARD THERE WAS PIZZA.
A **FREE MEAL** IS A FREE MEAL.

MANY YEARS LATER IN DOG HEAVEN (A.K.A. CAT HELL)...
PATIENCE MONTY, PATIENCE. CLIMB THE **ALPHA DOG** LADDER.
THE END

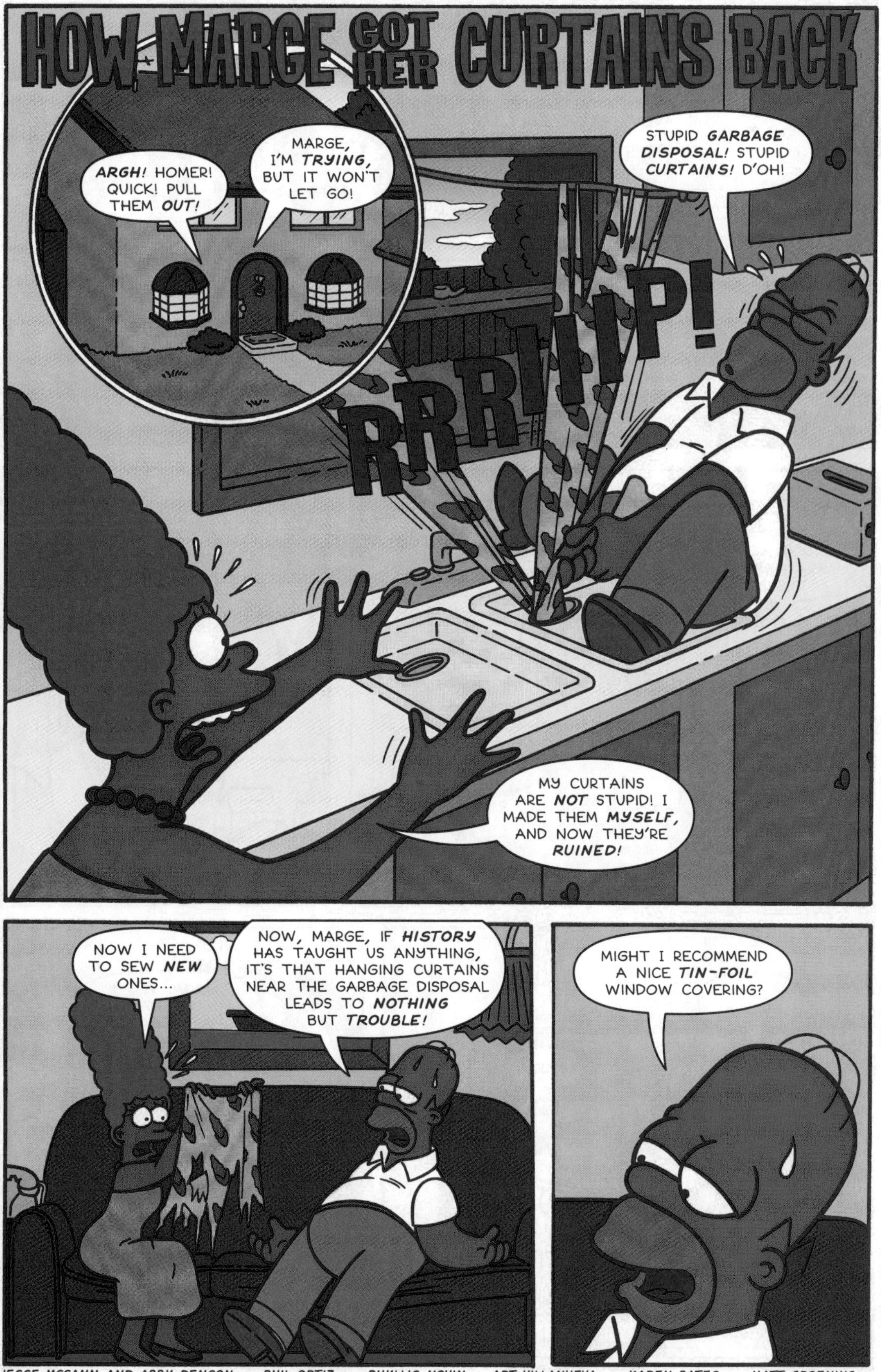

HOW MARGE GOT HER CURTAINS BACK

ARGH! HOMER! QUICK! PULL THEM OUT!

MARGE, I'M TRYING, BUT IT WON'T LET GO!

STUPID GARBAGE DISPOSAL! STUPID CURTAINS! D'OH!

RRRIIIIP!

MY CURTAINS ARE NOT STUPID! I MADE THEM MYSELF, AND NOW THEY'RE RUINED!

JESSE MCCANN AND ABBY DENSON STORY · *PHIL ORTIZ* PENCILS · *PHYLLIS NOVIN* INKS · *ART VILLANUEVA* COLORS · *KAREN BATES* LETTERS · *MATT GROENING* INTERIOR DECORATOR

I DIDN'T DO IT
THE BE SHARPS
LISA LIONHEART DOLLS
HRMMM! LOOKS LIKE THERE'S NOT ENOUGH MATERIAL LEFT OVER FROM THE LAST SEVERAL TIMES THEY WERE DESTROYED.

MARGE, DO WE HAVE ANY CHOCOLATE-FLAVORED BEER?
THERE'S NO SUCH THING, HOMER.
I'M GOING TO ORDER MORE OF THAT CORNCOB DESIGN FABRIC, SO WE'LL HAVE NEW CURTAINS AS SOON AS POSSIBLE!

AH, WHAT'S THE HURRY, MARGE? IT'S NOT LIKE THEY'RE GOOD FOR ANYTHING BUT A DECORATION.

OH, REALLY?
YIKES!

TWO WEEKS LATER...
HOORAY! MY CORNCOB MATERIAL HAS ARRIVED!

DOO-DEE-
DOO-DEE-
DOO!
HRMMM...

ANOTHER TWO WEEKS LATER...
DOO-DEE-
DOO-DEE-
DOO!
HRMMM...

TWO WEEKS AFTER THAT...
DOO-DEE-
DOO-DEE-
DOO!
HRMMM!
CORN PALACE

WE'VE GOT TO GO TO THE "WE'VE GOT WEAVES" WAREHOUSE IN OGDENVILLE. THEY'RE BOUND TO HAVE THAT FABRIC!
BUT MARGE! I'VE NEARLY PERFECTED MY CHOCO-BEER!

YOU, TOO, SANTA'S LITTLE HELPER.
URK!

SCREEEEEEE!

OGDENVILLE...
HRMMM. CLOSE BUT NO CIGAR.
OGDENVILLE! HAH! THE PEOPLE HERE ARE SO FULL OF THEMSELVES! OOOH! I'M FROM OGDENVILLE! I AM SOOO SPECIAL!

OH, DEAR! PLEASE EXCUSE ME.
UUUH!
BUMP!

SEE WHAT I MEAN! THE PEOPLE HERE ARE SO RUDE WITH THEIR HIGH AND MIGHTY OGDENVILLEAN ATTITUDES!
OH, HUSH. WE WON'T BE HERE MUCH LONGER!

MAY I HELP YOU MISS?
YES. WE'RE LOOKING FOR FABRIC WITH A CORNCOB PATTERN.
COULD YOU PLEASE WAIT HERE A MOMENT? I'LL BE RIGHT BACK.

ANOTHER "CONTACT" IS HERE. SHE KNEW THE CODE WORD: "CORNCOB".
VERY GOOD. PROCEED WITH PHASE TWO.

YOUR INSTRUCTIONS ARE IN THIS ENVELOPE. IT CONTAINS ALL THE INFORMATION YOU NEED. YOU MUST DESTROY IT IMMEDIATELY AFTER READING IT.
OH, MY! CORNCOB FABRIC MUST BE GETTING VERY POPULAR!

AAAAH!
FREEZE! FBI! YOU'RE UNDER ARREST FOR SELLING BLACK MARKET ITEMS!

RUN! AND DON'T LET THEM TAKE YOU ALIVE!
BLAM!
BLAM!
BLAM!
AARGH! MY EYES!

BLAM!
BLAM!
EEEEK! I TOLD YOU THESE OGDEN-VILLE PEOPLE WERE INSANE!
BLAM!

WHAT'LL WE DO? WE CAN'T GO TO THE OGDENVILLE POLICE! THEY'RE SURE TO BE CORRUPT!
I DON'T KNOW WHAT'S HAPPENING, HOMER, BUT THERE'S A TRAP DOOR UNDER HERE.

LOOK AT THIS PLACE! IT'S SOME KIND OF BLACK MARKET!
FORGET ABOUT THE BLACK MARKET, MARGE! LOOK AT ALL THE ILLEGAL STUFF THEY'RE SELLING!
CONTRABAND
GEMS
LET'S SEE WHAT'S IN THIS ENVELOPE...OH, GOOD GRIEF!
GREMLINS
CIGARS
MOONSHINE
BIG BLACK MARKET SALE! THIS SATURDAY ONLY!

I THINK WE LOST THEM, MARGE, BUT YOU NEVER CAN BE TOO SURE WHEN IT'S OGDENVI...

GASP! I DON'T BELIEVE IT!
UNCLE LEON'S OLD-FASHIONED CHOCO-BEER!
ON SALE HERE!

OH, HOMEY! AT LAST! THE PATTERN I NEED!
I'LL TAKE TWELVE YARDS!
FELONIOUS FABRICS
YOU HAVE TO BUY THE WHOLE THING, LADY. IT'S ALL OR NOTHIN'. SEVENTY BUCKS!

SOLD!

AND SO...
NOW THAT'S MORE LIKE IT!

MMMM... CHOCO-BEER!
MOM, DON'T YOU THINK THESE OUTFITS ARE A LITTLE COR...
DON'T EVEN SAY IT!
UNCLE LEON'S OLD-FASHIONED CHOCO-
THE END